AWAY WITH WORDS

Young Writers' 16th Annual Poetry Competition

It is feeling and force of imagination that make us eloquent.

How can I not dream while writing? The blank page gives a right to dream.

YoungWriters

Poems From The South
Edited by Michelle Afford

 Young**Writers**

First published in Great Britain in 2007 by:
Young Writers
Remus House
Coltsfoot Drive
Peterborough
PE2 9JX
Telephone: 01733 890066
Website: www.youngwriters.co.uk

SB ISBN 978-1 84431 285 6

Foreword

This year, the Young Writers' *Away With Words* competition proudly presents a showcase of the best poetic talent selected from thousands of up-and-coming writers nationwide.

Young Writers was established in 1991 to promote the reading and writing of poetry within schools and to the young of today. Our books nurture and inspire confidence in the ability of young writers and provide a snapshot of poems written in schools and at home by budding poets of the future.

The thought, effort, imagination and hard work put into each poem impressed us all and the task of selecting poems was a difficult but nevertheless enjoyable experience.

We hope you are as pleased as we are with the final selection and that you and your family continue to be entertained with *Away With Words Poems From The South* for many years to come.

Contents

Emily Smith (13)	50
Peter Copplestone (11)	50
Georgina Hobbs (13)	51
Cassie Bellinger (12)	51
Aimèe Sheridan (13)	52
Kate Watts (11)	52
Kieran Gooding (12)	53
Bob Rush (12)	53
Patrick Zhang (13)	54
Lisa Bellairs (11)	55
Katie Bryant (12)	56
Jim Morgan (12)	57
Rebecca Drew (13)	57
Gwendolen Farrell (12)	58
Emma Thomas (13)	59
Lottie Davies (12)	60
Joshua Ravenscoft (12)	60
Lloyd Moore (13)	61
Shaun Wheatley (11)	61
Katie Cunningham (12)	62
Beth Wilde (13)	62
Chris Merrifield (12)	63
Tasha Bate (13)	63
Shannon Miller (13)	64
Danielle Smith (12)	64
Eleanor Perkin (12)	65
Matthew Cole (12)	65
Alex Butler (12)	66
Jenny Persson (12)	66
Megan O'Neil (12)	67
Kieran Miles (11)	67
Garrick Hill (12)	68
Sophie Thornton (11)	69
Charlotte Shemilt (12)	69
James Kivell (12)	70
Nick Feltham (12)	70
Jordan Cole (12)	71
Nathan Parfett (13)	71
Tom Morley (11)	72
Jimmy Williams (11)	72
Katherine Bryant (11)	73
Tom Wheeler (13)	73

Daniel Thompson (12)	74
Nicola Payne-Heard (12)	74
Joshua Sparrow (11)	75
Stacey Thomas (12)	75
Luke Wilson (12)	76
James Walker (12)	76
Kristina Beech (12)	77
David Sellars (13)	77
Tova Persson (12)	78
Sian Sycamore (12)	78
Amy Osborne (11)	79
Chloe Payton (12)	79
Rachel Lowson (12)	80
Kieran Parish (12)	80
Josh Danks (14)	81
Sally Sluggett (12)	81
Amy-Laura Dixon (11)	82
Roxanne Edwards (12)	82
Jack Whitfield (12)	83
Charlotte Balston (12)	83
Cheyenne Hardwick (12)	84
Kimberley Anstis (12)	84
Kim Holloway (12)	85
Katie Domingo (12)	85
Emily Wright (13)	86
Skye Davy (12)	86
Beth Hartley (12)	87
Becky Dawson (13)	87
Sammy Pettit (12)	88
Dom Clapton (12)	88
Lauren Meadows (12)	89
Courtney Ward (12)	89
Shannon Mannix (12)	90
Rebecca Piper (12)	91
Jade Kirkum (12)	92
Jack Parratt (12)	92
William Middleton (13)	93
Coreen Thorne (12)	93
Caitlin Quinn (12)	94
Jake Cartwright (13)	95
Holly Smale (12)	96
Matt Eusden (12)	97

Barnaby Simpson (13)	98
Jordan Davis (13)	98
Lauren Miller (12)	99
Matthew Whitefield (13)	99
Sophie Jenks (12)	100
Sophie English	101
Briony Smith (12)	102
Lola Thorpe (12)	103
Francesca Metherell (11)	104

Clyst Vale Community College, Exeter

Cicely Street-Mellor (13)	105

Colyton Grammar School, Colyton

Adam Ward (14)	106

East Court School For Dyslexia, Ramsgate

Dominic Williams-Stevens (13)	107
Sebastian Wilkins (13)	107
Sean Cragg (13)	108
Sam Draper (12)	109

Exeter School, Exeter

Robyn Lockyer (13)	110
Chris Clay (12)	110
Sam Jellard (12)	111
Sam Russell (13)	111
Alice Tolson (13)	112
Emily Kirk (13)	112
Bryony Mann (13)	113
Tom Pearson (13)	113
Cameron Starling (13)	113

Great Torrington School, Torrington

Charlotte Fanson (12)	114
Dean Folland (12)	114
Charlie Elliott (11)	115
Bethany Piper (12)	115
Melissa Troke (12)	116
Ruby Cockwill (12)	116

Shobika Mohamed (13)   141
Bethany Appleyard (12)   142
Alanah Mortlock (13)   143
Anna Westley (12)   144
Harriet Sands (13)   145
Celine Lee (13)   146
Geneviève Zane (13)   147
Olivia Smith (12)   148
Mina Thiraviyarajah (13)   148

St John's Catholic Comprehensive School, Gravesend
Alexandra Wheeler (14)   149

Slough Grammar School, Slough
Jass-preet Sohal (13)   150
Zahra Gain (13)   151
Sophie Long (13)   152
Alice Schmitz (13)   152
Gurneet Kaur Gill (13)   153
Vicknaraj Sahadevan (13)   153
Abu Miah (13)   154
Ekta Namas (13)   154
Isobel Byrne (13)   155
Symrath Virdee (13)   155
Arjan Singh Bains (12)   156
Lara Mackey (13)   157
James Wickens (13)   158
Amreen Dhanoya (13)   158
Hannah Wiltshire (14)   159
Arjun Jung (13)   159
Farhia Afzal (13)   160
William Wright (12)   160
Manraj Jhalli & Jaskaran Sandhu (13)   161
Pavindeep Randhawa (13)   161
Manveer Singh Chander (12)   162
Sahib Singh Dhillon (13)   162
Nicole Edwards (12)   163
Arif Javed (12)   164
Jack Glen (13)   164
Douglas Naylor (13)   165
Ela Berksoy (13)   165

The Oratory School, Reading

Tower House School, Paignton

The Poems

No One Cares

When Mum said she was pregnant,
I didn't know it would be like this;
No one seems to notice me,
I don't even get a goodnight kiss.

Everything's about the baby,
Is it a boy, is it a girl?
Yellow, pink, blue?
Does anybody really care?
All the baby's going to do is poo!

I even have to share my room,
Because our house is too small;
The baby has more stuff than me,
And he'll dribble over it all!

All my friends' baby siblings
Are cute, funny and sweet;
I know that won't be my baby,
He will not be petite.

I certainly hope it's not a boy,
That will be no fun;
With a girl at least we can shop and stuff,
Cos girls are number one!

I guess this might not be all that bad,
She may be really cute;
It I tell Mum and Dad my problem,
That'll give this feeling the boot.

When I told Mum, she said sorry,
She claimed she didn't know;
I should have told her sooner,
Now the wait for the baby is going slow!

Aisling Murphy (11)
Babington House School, Chislehurst

Life

What is the meaning of life?
The beautiful flowers, the wonderful world,
The sunset by the rippling sea,
The animals that we all love so
Or care, trust with a loving family?

Why are we here in life?
Life is a brilliant dream, life is the whole wide world,
God brought us to life on Earth,
Pain, anger, happiness and faith
Or science for the need to discover.

Why is there cruelty in life?
For justice, for no honest, truthful reason,
For people do not care for others,
For people think they are better than the rest
Or life is how it should be.

What is life?
Life is a gift, life is a saint,
Life is religious and for worship,
Life should be honoured and praised forever
Life is poetry, to express your emotions.

Sophie Hoque (11)
Babington House School, Chislehurst

Memories

M y favourite memories always make me smile
E very time I think of them I laugh for a while
M e and my friend having so much fun
O n holiday we played in the hot summer sun
R iding our bikes to our hearts' content
 I n shops we bought sweets until our money was spent
E leven years old with the world at our feet
S o many happy days, it was one big treat!

Sophie Presley (11)
Babington House School, Chislehurst

Young Writers - Away With Words Poems From The South

If Only

I lost my voice in a nasty car accident,
My friends won't talk to me anymore,
But then again,
I can't talk to them either.

I feel lonely and sad,
I want to be able to join in,
My parents say my so-called friends have no feelings,
I don't believe them.

I just want to be back to myself again,
Once more, as least I'd have friends.
Stupid accident . . . I hate it!
I'm being bullied.

Have you ever been bullied?
It's upsetting, people keep making fun of me.
I have one special friend, he's always there for me,
But he gets teased because he's my friend, by my side.

'Samuel is a loser, stupid sign language,' people say to me,
my friend Tom sticks up for me,
he gets teased too.
I wish I had my voice back.

If only I had put my seat belt on,
The time I got into the car.
Crash! Bang! Ouch!
I would never have lost my voice.

Ruby Middleton (10)
Babington House School, Chislehurst

Observing

Observing for millions of years
On this dull Earth.
So before I die here,
I tell you my story.

Here since time began
Observing, observing,
The human race,
Watching, watching.

So now I tell you,
Your fatal mistakes:
Greed, anger, arrogance,
Violence, jealousy, all unnoticed.

So those are my conclusions,
From noting, noting
The human race,
Examining, examining.

Observing for millions of years
On this dull Earth.
So before I die here,
I give you warning:
These mistakes will lead to your deaths!

Erica Douglas (11)
Babington House School, Chislehurst

The Refugee

I took a flight not knowing why,
Sleeping most of the way.
Why did we have to leave home?
Why was it not safe to stay?

Suddenly our plane landed,
We alighted quickly but carefully,
Wondering if we were stranded,
But soon discovered we were here.

The next thing I knew we were standing,
Standing on the doorstep of a block of flats.
People looked at us - not understanding,
Who, why we were here?

I didn't have an answer for them,
But then I suddenly did.
I stood out, like an abnormal gem,
An emerald in a pile of diamonds.

I suppose you are now wondering why I'm a refugee,
It can be complicated, but for me it's not.
It's simple why people usually flee,
Because of a war, a war, *a war!*

Alex Ball (10)
Babington House School, Chislehurst

I Wish I Had A Voice

I cannot talk
All my friends walk away from me
It's not my fault

When I get bullied
I cannot say anything
Because I'm mute

Expressing my feelings is hard
No one understands me
How sad it is to be like me

I wish I had a voice
To tell my family how much I love them
Unfortunately I can't, because I'm mute.

Diyora Shadijanova (11)
Babington House School, Chislehurst

Road Of Destiny

I walk on this lonely road
With the moonlight guiding me,
I walk to follow my dreams

But then the rain starts to descend,
With a strong wind pushing me back,
And a fog hiding the path

I hear a voice from the sky
Telling me to keep marching,
To always follow my dreams

Soon the rain will cease to fall,
And the mist will fade away
To reveal a brighter day

I continue my journey,
I'll walk to follow my dreams,
On the road of destiny.

Myriam Raja (14)
Baylis Court School, Slough

Why

Why does my heart skip a beat when your eyes interlock with mine?
Why is it when you smile at me, my worries dissolve and I'm fine?

Why can't I wake up one day without hearing the echo of your voice?
Why is it you say you're in love with her?
Why can't you make a choice?

Why is it when I see her, my body rebels and I start shaking?
Is it rage, anger; or is it my heart breaking?

Why do you tempt and tease me with the touch of your skin?
Why can you not discover what I feel for you within?

Why can't I continue with my life, burn the memories like a flame?
Why is it so hard to move on and open my heart again?

Why can't I approach you to open up and reveal
How much I need you in my life, and what I really feel?

Why is it when you hold me I want to hold on forever?
Why did I ever think that we could be together?

Why can't I let you go, is it your love or affection?
Why can't I confront you, is it the fear of rejection?

I was a prisoner of your act; you were the core of my pain.
Why must I live in regret and not love another again?

A man you call yourself, an element of God's creation,
Yet you let me suffer in doubt and humiliation.

I was a girl, now a woman. Was oblivious, now I see.
Why I was hypnotised and let you have control of me.

I just want to know this one question,
Before my heart crumbles in despair,
Where were you when I was hurt, when I needed you there?

She's won your heart now, so why do I sense defeat?
Is it because without you my life, my soul is incomplete?

I'm just a heart-broken woman, watching time go by.
I just want to, need to, know, why me? Why?

Stephanie Gumbs (15)
Baylis Court School, Slough

The Modern World

Some people want you to be something
Other people want you to be something completely different
So who am I?
I'm not an Asian Muslim girl or a simple British girl

Today, tomorrow, it's all the same, day in, day out
I'm a Muslim girl living in a modern world
Filled with practicalities, rules and society

There is nothing simple about me, I am who I am
This world is made up of who we are
If there were just one type of person here
Then this world would be so dull

People's culture, traditions, growing up with those around us
People are always debating
About which has the greater impact on a person's life
Nature or nurture

If your belief is strong you shall remain strong
Media news, peer pressure
People here show off their figures, going out with boys
Lying, cheating, it's not the right way
It's the weakness of this world

If you let yourself forget who you are
And act like a clone of someone who has no strength of character
Then you'll only hurt yourself and those who love you

So many people in this world, take one look at you and think
A Muslim/Asian girl, they're no good
Their kind make trouble, they don't belong here
So what are they doing here?

You may think your actions account for much but you are so wrong
If you let people think you're no good, trouble, then that's the image
You portray for the rest of the world
And people think all of us are no good, troublemakers
Your actions count for so much

But if you do something good, set yourself apart
Show the world how great you can be
We're not worthless, you may not be bad news

But because of someone else's actions, people think you are,
Don't waste your time, think, speak your mind
And don't let people keep that impression of you

Show them who we really are, always remember you're out there
Representing us as well
You can change the world, make such a difference
In this modern world.

Semera Saddique (15)
Baylis Court School, Slough

You Say What She Says

One day I'm with you,
The next with her,
Either way, I'm with both of you.
You're both exactly the same,
You play the same game
And sing the same song.
She says what you say,
You say what she says,
You both say the same,
You play the same game
And sing the same song.
You say one thing, she says another,
She says one thing you say another.
It's funny for a time
Until you figure out the crime.
Who exactly is responsible?
Either way's the same.
It's the same reason
And you both want to end the same.
You think what she thinks,
She thinks what you think.
So why do you both think?
What is your thinking?
I know this isn't fun,
But, you're not the only one.

Firdos Bhatti (15)
Baylis Court School, Slough

Always Alone

I'm always alone
No one's ever there for me
No one cares about what happens to me
No one knows what I go through
No one knows how I feel
All I want is for someone to love me
All I want is for someone to care
All I want is for someone to hug me
And to tell me they'll always be there
To tell me that I'm not on my own
To tell me they'll never break my heart
To tell me that they'll always stand by my side
To tell me that they'll never break me apart
But I know that won't happen
I know it's all a dream
I know it's what I wish for, I know I'm on my own
I know no one loves me, I know no one cares
And that's why I'm dying
I'm dying from the inside
All I ever do is cry
Why can't I just die?
I always pray for death
But my prayers are never accepted
So I'm going to do it now
I'm going to kill myself
Even though I know it is wrong
I know it's a sin
But I can't help it
What's the point of staying alive
When I'm always alone?

Zaeema Jabeen Hussain (15)
Baylis Court School, Slough

Your Feelings

Your heart.
Life is here once and then it's over
What really matters is what's in your heart.
You can be a star, then fall and become dust.
It's all about the choices you make.
The mysteries you solve and the problems you run into.
You have a key within you and that key can unlock anything.
Whether it is finding the person you love or solving a problem.
The key is your heart.

Dreams.
What's in your head only you know.
It's a secret place which only you can enter.
It's where all your memories are
and special things which are your dreams.
You find your dreams at night and think about them all day.
You sometimes wish your dreams could come true,
or wish they would go away.
You can fulfil your dreams.
They can be good or bad,
That's why dreams are wonderful things.

Happiness.
Happiness is something we all pray for.
We beg God for it.
We have it all around us, we all need happiness.
It can be getting a new car, passing an exam, or even a new baby.
Happiness can be anything.
To have happiness is to give it away.
Giving it is the greatest feeling.

Faaizah Rafiq (11)
Baylis Court School, Slough

Meaning Of Life

The question I ask is, why are we here?
There are so many questions but no answers.
I am a human being, superior to all,
I have the right to kill, to punish, educate,
To love, drink, to pollute, to steal.
And yet I don't know the difference
Between right and wrong.

The question I ask is, why are we here?
Who decides what I do with my life?
Myself, my parents, God who is superior to all?
We destroy other lives, is it to show power?
Who are we to do this?
Doesn't everyone have the same rights in the eyes of God?

The question I ask is, why are we here?
I say this world will be doomed, because of the way we live,
Polluted by us.
Once Earth was Heaven, slowly turned evil,
With our intelligence, science, discoveries.
There will be an end to mankind,
We can't rule forever.
When you think you've got somewhere,
There are so many more stairs to climb.
Why is this I ask?

The question I ask is, why are we here?
There are so many questions but no answers.
Science we fear and love,
And say it helps us understand the world,
But then why do we still believe in God?

Kasturi Sothirajah (13)
Bentley Wood High School, Stanmore

Why Don't You Try To Give A Name To This Poem

The world today is meant to be the best,
Where war and hate are forever put to rest.
But still that sadness hits us anon,
When we realise the world does not stand as one.

The people who starve every day,
And in the night they always pray,
For it to be better, surely they did not deserve this,
This pain and suffering in the abyss?

The countries that do not care for none,
About what evil they have caused or done,
They pollute the world's beautiful atmosphere,
And kill their children's future, which ever draws near.

The everyday people who you think you know,
Turn out to be convicts and when this is so,
We turn on each other to inflict anger and hate,
And cause riots in the street which were once nice and safe.

The masked strangers who come,
Grab children and run,
Who they lock away, making them all alone,
Make parents cautious around their homes.

The little children who cry for love,
When parents leave them and away they shove,
The children that should be cared for the most,
But end up unloved and turned into ghosts.

After all this, how can you say
That this is the world we should be in today,
Where people don't love and their anger roasts,
When the time is now when we should love the most?

We should pull together and we should show them.
Why don't you try and give a name to this poem?

Meesha Patel (13)
Bentley Wood High School, Stanmore

A Friendship Poem

A friend is a treasure of the rarest find
A person who stays with you in your heart and mind
A flower that will bloom because of the warmth one gives it
A friend is forever, a loving gift
A friend is the candlelight where there is darkness
A person to turn to when nobody will listen
A bird of sweet songs and a breeze that drifts
A friend is forever, a loving gift
A friend is the sun that shines down on ones life
A person of honesty and heart-warming advice
A butterfly that expresses it colours and bliss
A friend is forever, a loving gift
A friend is a diary in which one can keep secrets
A person who will be there when you are in need
A hug that feels sweeter than a kiss
A friend is forever, a loving gift.

Melissa Tsaparis (13)
Bentley Wood High School, Stanmore

Is There God?

Is there a spirit in the sky
Who decides whether we live or die?
Is there a person up in Heaven,
Beating the clouds to drum bass seven?

Is there a person making it rain, making it snow,
Who constructs the rhythm and makes the flow?
Does He choose whether we win or lose,
Or if we fall and get a permanent bruise?

Is there a spirit choosing the path we take
Or is it just destiny and fate?
Is there a person looking down on us,
Listening to our problems and our fuss?

Please tell me *now!* I need your help.
Is there a god to hear me scream and yelp!

Damaris Downie-Solomon (14)
Bentley Wood High School, Stanmore

Argh!

What's going on?
First men, then women and elderly, now children!
A ghost haunting everyone's life . . .
But no one cares.
I do! What's the point?
Argh!
This ghost is around to steal innocent lives,
Using guns, bombs and knives.
What is the point?
Argh!
It's useless, violent conflict between a group of selfish leaders.
Why do normal people have to pay the price?
What is the point?
Argh!
People killing . . . people dying,
People taking people's lives.
The world is tearing apart.
What is the point?

Houda Basma (13)
Bentley Wood High School, Stanmore

Guju Veggies

I'm a big bateta, fat and round,
Where I come from is beneath the ground.

Unlike no other veggies or fruits,
If you leave me in the dark, I start growing shoots.

I am often brought over in big, long ships,
They cut me and fire me, turn me into chips.

There's only one veggie that's better than me,
And that's the amazing, most fabulous doongri.

Shyama Sodha (13)
Bentley Wood High School, Stanmore

Food Is Yummy

Food is yummy
Food is great
Food fulfils your needs

Ice cream, chocolate
Jelly on a plate
Food is food, it's great!

Eating food is the best time of the day,
I start with chips and just get carried away.
Seafood, fast food, Indian, roast,
Orange juice in the morning followed by Marmite toast.
Dippy egg with soldiers is the ultimate best,
But spaghetti Bolognese bets the rest.

Food is yummy
Food is great
Food fulfils your needs

Burger, fries
Salad on a plate
Food is food, it's great!

Kailee Marks (14)
Bentley Wood High School, Stanmore

Roses

Roses are as red as blood,
As pretty as a flower,
As elegant as a swan,
As delicate as the first snowflake in winter,
Roses are for everyone!

Roses are red,
Roses are precious,
Roses are delicate,
Roses are romantic,
Roses are for everyone!

Shivani Patel (12)
Bentley Wood High School, Stanmore

The Truth About Love

A broken heart cries with pain,
and figures rush around,
she feels her mind can't take this strain,
so she stays silent, not a sound.

In love, true happiness is found,
but soon hurt and heartbreak start,
she weeps, she cries,
inside she dies,
a million tears roll down.

She blames herself for all that's done,
he laughed and went away,
he was the light, her life, her sun,
and she didn't get a say.

Time heals, moments pass,
and photographs bring memories of the past,
as tears fall down like hail and rain,
she knew moments wouldn't last,
she knows she'll never love again.

Mairi MacArthur (14)
Bentley Wood High School, Stanmore

I Love Noise

I love noise!
The crash of thunder, the crackle of fire,
The happy cry of an Ebay buyer.
The roar of a lion, the bleat of lambs,
The bangs of babies playing with pans,
The whoosh of wind, the splash of rain,
The echoing footsteps down the lane.
Rough or smooth, quiet or loud,
I feel like floating on a cloud.
I love noise!

Zoe Beattie (13)
Bentley Wood High School, Stanmore

Anne Bonny

In Dublin a man named Johnny,
Met a girl know as Anne Bonny,
She was as wild and as unruly as the sea,
But as beautiful as a cherry tree.

She caught his eye,
Johnny's love for her grew day and night,
He offered Anne a journey around the seven seas,
Anne always dreamt of seeing exotic kingdoms.

The journey to paradise took a different twist,
She fell in love with Roger Nist,
The pirates and Anne raided islands' treasures,
And drank rum in great measures.

Johnny was in ire, went back to Ireland,
Became a fishmonger,
Like his father before,
His love for Anne was no more.

Sophya Polevaya (13)
Bentley Wood High School, Stanmore

The Endless Fight

The heart will cry.
The soul will mourn.
But the body won't change,
it won't feel anything.

It will smile and show,
that nothing is wrong,
but inside the soul will curdle up
and will urge death.

No one knows the fighting
between the soul, heart and body,
no one can call peace
once one has already died.

Fatemah Soniji (14)
Bentley Wood High School, Stanmore

The Moon

O Moon,
you are really bright,
you are a diamond.
You light up the starry night,
the nights, which are peaceful and silent.

O Moon,
you are like the sun,
but you come out at night.
You make me feel so happy,
because you're a beautiful sight.

O Moon,
you are so dazzling,
which is very true.
You're the best thing I've ever seen,
because there's nothing like you.

Ume Kulsoom Akbar (12)
Bentley Wood High School, Stanmore

Emotions

You try and try, but yet you fail
Only you alone can tell
How much it hurts deep inside
And how it ruins all your pride

You watch and stare as people win
You then feel like poking yourself with a pin
For you know you could have tried harder
Because you know that you are a fighter

So you gather courage
And remember, that determination is your friend
With determination only you can tell
What the future holds for you and others as well.

Buki Fatuga (13)
Bentley Wood High School, Stanmore

I Love The Seasons

Winter is the best season in the year
It's the only time you can snuggle up with your bear
Little cotton balls fall from the sky
Santa Claus might pass you by

Autumn has rain and sun
It makes the weather fun
Leaves fall from the trees
Piled up to my knees

Spring is the time of peace
While I sit under a tree with my niece
Birds sing a song
All day long

Summer is time for play
Which I like to do all day
My friends and I sit under the evening sky
If I told you I hated the seasons it would be a lie.

Sonal Maroo (13)
Bentley Wood High School, Stanmore

Flowers

Flowers are pretty,
Flowers are bright,
Flowers are colourful
And they smell really nice.

Flowers are rainbows up in the sky
Flowers are paints,
Flowers are different,
That's why they're special to us.

Flowers are important to our human life,
Flowers grow in different shapes and heights,
And they are beautiful
Just like us.

Nishda Naufal (12)
Bentley Wood High School, Stanmore

O Broccoli

Broccoli, O broccoli
Your name makes me go all yucky
I hate thee so much
Yet my mummy makes me eat thee so much

Broccoli, O broccoli
You look so soft and crinkly
I hate thee so much
Yet you have those that love you so much

Broccoli, O broccoli
You belong to the cabbage family
I hate thee so much
Yet we don't have salad as much

Broccoli, O broccoli
You may help with heart disease quickly
I hate thee so much
Yet again, I may be wrong just as much

Broccoli, O broccoli
You may be liked by all young eventually
I am sure not that I hate thee so much
Yet again I may take time to love thee much.

Payal Karia (13)
Bentley Wood High School, Stanmore

The Dark Monster

In darkness
anything can creep up on you,
in darkness,
is there really anything to do?
When the lights go out
and when the sun goes down,
when your smile disappears
and is replaced by a frown,
that's when the dark monster
will come around.

Katrina Stocker (12)
Bentley Wood High School, Stanmore

The Magic Box

(Based on 'Magic Box' by Kit Wright)

I will put in my box . . .
A lovely, warm taste of Asian curry,
A smile of a newborn baby,
A glimmer of sunshine beaming down on my sunlit face,
A sound of the first note in a new song,
A glamorous supermodel with a skinny figure.

I will put in my box . . .
A shimmering star reflecting the warm, sunlit ocean,
The planet Saturn showing off his glamorous rings,
A fast silver Ferrari speeding down the vast motorway,
A colourful, dazzling, multicoloured rainbow.

I will put in my box . . .
A dazzling Indian sari, so soft and silky,
A marvellous dream, never to forget,
An old school photo of my loving, previous schools,
A deep green jungle with slithery snakes,
A snow-white horse galloping through a fresh pine forest.

I will put in my box . . .
A cratered moon, full of glorious cheese
And excellent bedtime stories,
Thierry Henry in the challenging Premiership League,
Scoring a short and sweet goal,
A book full of swirling poems full of imagination,
A kaleidoscope that shows shiny illusions of all kinds of triangles.

I will put in my box . . .
A scrumptious, finger-licking chocolate cake,
A blood-red rose with blood-red petals,
An enjoyable birthday party for everyone, young and old,
A new year with new resolutions with new thoughts and feelings,
A peaceful country with no one to disturb the love in your heart,
The end of a heart-filling poem, ready to be published.

What will you put in your box?
I've told you what I would put in mine!

Rianna Thompson (13)
Bentley Wood High School, Stanmore

Misinterpreted

She needed to step out of the scene,
Needed to realise the fault within her brain,
She needed to count from one to ten,
Life for her was only an emotional train.

She backed away and took a seat,
Just to realise her life had gone down the gutter,
She could no longer withstand the pain,
Of knowing her fate was as slippery as butter.

Everything and everyone she had ever loved had gone,
What could she say?
Nothing was the same, she was immune,
How could she take the pain away?

Frantically trying to pin-point the exact fault,
She couldn't take so much of this strife,
She tried so hard to act so normal,
She wondered if reality existed in her double life.

She never knew the real person she was,
Every day she lived was another painful lie,
A vortex only she created for herself,
A vortex she couldn't flee, however hard she tried.

And she couldn't help but live in the past,
But hopefully things would change for her,
Maybe one day things would click into place,
And life would not result in such a dark blur.

But still she unwillingly stands to this day,
Labelled as a happy-go-lucky sort of girl,
Even though not a soul realises the truth -
That this unknown girl doesn't belong
in this distorted, shameful world.

Crystal Blackburn (13)
Bentley Wood High School, Stanmore

Every Minute

Every minute a child dies
But we question why
Because they suffer from malnutrition
The food we have and throw away
Poor people don't even get two meals a day.

Every minute a child dies
But we question why
Because bombs, guns and violence kill
Despair from adults
Screams from children
Now some people don't even have the will to live.

Every minute a child dies
But we question why
Because there is no shelter for them to live under
So they aren't even protected from the thunder
Throats parched
Arms and legs dangle helplessly
And their hopes and dreams battered and bruised
Their dreams are broken before they can even pursue them.

Every minute a child dies
But we question why
Because we don't help enough
Cough after cough
Broken arm after broken leg
Screams after fights
Broken dreams after broken hearts.

Every minute a child dies
But we question what we can do
We can help as a community, as a nation
Change broken dreams to inspiration
Change inevitable death to hope
Change broken hearts to mended ones
Change no future to a bright future
Change a person's life
The greatest gift anyone can give.

Krupa Mehta (14)
Bentley Wood High School, Stanmore

Amazing Animals

I travelled to the amazing sights of Asia,
To hear the mighty blow of the elephant,
To see the giant panda eat effortlessly,
But there was nothing to be seen and silence.

I travelled to the amazing sights of the Arctic,
To feel the snow-white fur on the polar bear,
To catch a glimpse of the sneaky snow leopard,
But I didn't catch a glimpse nor touch fur.

I travelled to the amazing sights of Africa,
To hear the monkeys making music,
To watch the terrific tiger,
But I didn't hear the music or see the tiger.

I stood there in the middle of the jungle,
I stood there in the middle of the snow,
I stood there in the middle of the rainforest,
But I heard nothing, saw nothing, felt nothing.

What was this?
Where was I?
Was it a rainbow without any colours,
Or a flower without any petals?

Then I looked down at my ivory necklace,
Remembered the bamboo shoots in my meal last night,
Felt the white fur on my scarf,
And saw the tiger fur on my bag.

It was me, my fault, I had killed the animals.

Azelea Rushd (14)
Bentley Wood High School, Stanmore

What Is Love?

Love feels like angels carrying me to the heavens,
Love feels like your heart and body are warm,
Love feels like you are complete,
Love feels like we are one.

Love looks like the joining of two people,
Love looks like the sun and the moon,
They work together, yet they are different,
Love looks like nature,
It takes time to develop,
To be what it is supposed to be,
Love looks like an honest smile.

Love is confusing,
Love is trust,
Love is unmeasurable,
Love is a flower which grows stronger every day.

Amnah Nadeem (13)
Bentley Wood High School, Stanmore

About The Boy

There's this boy I think about all the time.
I wish that I could say he's mine.
I write his name all over my stuff,
Book, bags, folders too.
Sometimes I think that I'm a fool.

I think about the good points of the boy,
He's charming, sweet, funny too,
But I'd like to get to know him more,
His habits, if they're good or bad.
I'll always cheer him up when sad,
Then one day the boy will reach out his hand,
He'll know he's found the right girl.

Jereca Tafari (12)
Bentley Wood High School, Stanmore

What Is Life To Me . . .

Have you ever wondered what life is?
Ever thought what the meaning of life is?
Ever wondered what life is to you?

To me, life,
Is like a never-resting soul,
Is a never-ending destination.
Is like a path with a start not a stop,
Is like a long Tube train with many carriages.
That is what I think of life.

Life is a journey from birth to death,
Life is rough, never smooth,
Many problems come but with a solution.
Life is a calendar which carries on
But won't stop until the right time comes.
Life is a clock with minutes, hours and seconds,
Passing through without hesitation.
That is what I think of life.

Seema Bharadia (13)
Bentley Wood High School, Stanmore

Love

Love is as white as a dove,
resting in my heart.
Love tastes like a moonbeam,
shining through the night.
Love smells like the cologne on your neck,
every time I reach up.
Love sounds like the melody
of our voices together.
Love feels like a never-ending journey,
on the stairway of destiny.

Sruthi Praveen (13)
Bentley Wood High School, Stanmore

Sister Dearest

Is that Grace . . . my sister?
Wow! She looks nothing like me!
Her eyes sparkle so bright,
Her Afro hair reminds me of cotton candy.
Her beautiful soft, smooth skin.
How is she my sister?

Every time I touch her soft cheeks it feels like cotton balls.
Her smile cures me from pain.
She's like no one else, she's unique.
She's got a great spirit
And she is such a frisky girl.

The way she kicks her legs makes me laugh my lungs out.
I always think of what she might be in future.
An athlete, a ballerina, a dancer, a model, what might she be?

Her giggles are cuter than top fashion designers' clothes.
She truly is the swan of the family.

Barbara Ahenkorah (13)
Bentley Wood High School, Stanmore

Friends!

Your friends are always there for you
They never let you down
They will never ever make you frown

You talk on the phone day and night
And laugh about everything in sight
Friends make you laugh and smile
They always make it worth your while

They are there to comfort you
To listen to you and support you
When life becomes rough and tough

Life without friends is impossible
They are the people that know you best
Friends are special!

Hajin Shekany (12)
Bentley Wood High School, Stanmore

The Monster

Boom! Boom! Boom! Boom!
Can you hear the beast of doom?
Lock your doors, shut the blinds
He's coming and won't care what he finds.

Boom! Boom! Boom! Boom!
Can you hear the beast of doom?
His venomous fur and putrid claws
Are nothing compared to his carnivorous jaws.

Boom! Boom! Boom! Boom!
Can you hear the beast of doom?
He'll stop at nothing to find the one
That makes his blood boil like a machine gun.

Boom! Boom! Boom! Boom!
Can you hear the beast of doom?
Lock your doors, shut the blinds
He's coming and won't care what he finds.

Nadine Almanasfi (13)
Bentley Wood High School, Stanmore

Love

Love is a rainy day, with no emotion but sadness,
Love is like a piece of burnt toast, sour and bitter,
Love is like smoke that you cough and choke on,
Love is like a sad morning, just dull with nothing to smile about,
Love is an ambulance coming your way!
Love is a sad emotion that hurts you!

Charmi Vastani (12)
Bentley Wood High School, Stanmore

Somewhere There's Another World

Oh, sweet tender breeze
Brushing upon my cheeks
Like soft, motherly fingertips
Wiping innocent tears
Paddling your way through the fields
Blowing dandelions at my heels
You dance to my will.

Fluttering hummingbirds
Revealing unread poesy and words
Merrily, do me accompany
Through my exquisite journey;
Away, I fly upon the hills
Swiftly I jump from tree to tree
Quietly I share my secrets with the wind
Passionately I drift my life to the sea
Lovingly I hug my little angels bringing me a treat.

Away . . . swiftly, quietly, passionately and lovingly
I lead a fine life
Where the heart feels
The wound heals
By itself my secret seals
I kiss goodday to the moon and sun
For time falters and here remains the fun
An irretrievable moment is lived forever
While in harmony creatures live together.

And laying my head against a pillow of thornless rose
Carrying fresh fragrance to my nose
On a green velvet grass in numberless layers
Of shiny woollen quilt, I give a grin of priceless praise
Then loosen myself to the gaze
Upon the timeless sky suffused with stars in my eyes
But oh, how the panorama fades, how it dies
As the drowsy me
Falls deep asleep.

Awake, ablaze
To find myself to be
When I can't seem to find me
I flinch in panic, in agony
I decry to the deity
Why am I back to reality?
Where nature is just for nailing
Emotions left out in the rain soaking
Washed away is my freedom by a huge tsunami
In La Fournaise's magma is disposed serenity.

No such thing as harmony
Just misery and poverty
And the fear of World War III
No dandelions at my heels
No breeze dancing to my will
Instead, bloodstained glasses on the floor
Throbs at the door.

My heart is bleeding
My soul is pleading
But everything's deceiving
Thus, this is where I come from
Nowhere like where I would like to be from
My fate's seam is done
Yet still I live
As I embrace my sweetest dreams with ecstasy
And oh sweet, tender breeze
My only hope in bringing jolly mirth
At long last to my world; Earth.

Kritika Treebhoohun (14)
Bentley Wood High School, Stanmore

War Is A Time . . .

If we ask anyone if they are for a war,
You will find they will say no.
Ask yourself why and maybe you will know the answer,
But if you still can't figure out why,
Then I will tell you.

War is a time of hate,
When people are parted from their loved ones.
Children suffer from hunger,
With nothing but death written in their fate.

War is a time when parents have nowhere to go,
They have to feed their family.
It is a bad time to search for food,
Especially when morale is low.

War is a time when people are killed,
Mines buried underground hurt the enemy.
Children walk over them every day,
Against their own will.

War is a time when innocent individuals are hurt,
Either injured or killed by accident or on purpose.
Hospitals are full of naïve people,
No food to eat, not even a chance to wear a shirt.

War is a time when people fight,
For a little reason becomes major.
As countries join the war becomes bigger,
Something that started from a spark turns into a fright.

We can stop this war,
By working together and winning.
We can patch up broken hearts,
Change agonising screams into singing larks.
We are the people that can fulfil broken dreams,
Bring together families and work together as a team.
We can feed the homeless and poor,
This is our chance to open a new door.
We are the people that will change the future,
All we need to do is work together.

Vandini Patel (14)
Bentley Wood High School, Stanmore

The Garden Of Eden

The pale blue sky runs in front of me,
It is like an everlasting universe on top of imperfect humans,
Full of hatred, jealousy and sadness.
A hope,
A wish,
What does it bring?
I wonder if wishes become stars
And hopes make the sky its pearly blue.
My wish becomes a dream and I am standing in clouds,
Wishing I were higher and higher until I reach the sun.
Its warmth burns my heart and I become full of anger,
I start by cutting all the trees and end by polluting the water.
I am as imperfect as a human can be,
I am as sad and jealous as my brain will let me be.
I want the world for me,
Fame, money and love.
What is the point of sharing,
When not even your friends will share with you?
Why are people cursed with a big heart
That gives and gives until empty?
How can people kill without feeling guilty?
Why is this world so imperfect?
Can't we live in a big garden called the world?
A garden full of living trees, full of smiling people,
Full of love, full of happiness,
Around our garden is a fence and on it in big gold letters,
The Garden of Eden.

Pauline Joskin (14)
Bentley Wood High School, Stanmore

The Greatest Gift

It holds me in an eternal embrace;
Sometimes comforting, warm
But at other times it makes me face
The cold reality of the world's true form.

A companion forever in my loneliness,
An unrelenting reminder that I am not alone.
I command it to let me drown in my distress,
But it knows I could not bear it if it were gone.

It gives my building foundations,
Where everyone else's have crumbled and some to a stop.
It gives my fishes the ocean,
Where the rest are living on their last drop.

I have the travel card to life's bus,
Whilst the others have to walk.
I have the guide to life's path which I completely trust,
And everyone else is left stranded in shock.

My companion has never deserted me,
It has never let the waters of life flow over my dam.
Its embrace has never crushed my body,
It is my religion, my Islam.

Nasreen Alihassan (14)
Bentley Wood High School, Stanmore

Jealousy

Jealousy is as green as the leaves on a rainy day.
Jealousy tastes like chocolate without sugar.
Jealousy smells like burning candle wax.
Jealousy looks like footprints on a snowy day.
Jealousy sounds like mice in a sewer.
Jealousy feels like you're being bullied by greed.

Joie Lou (13)
Bentley Wood High School, Stanmore

Lion

I lick my luscious lips,
As fresh meat stumbles upon my territory,
My heart races as my adrenaline pumps,
This is my prey,
This is my lunch.

The sun beats down on my rough coat,
I swing back my thick, golden mane,
And tear across the leafy plain,
Like a strip of beaming light.

I leap into the empty air,
With the bare wind whipping my hair,
A subtle attack I had prepared,
But now I am not even scared.

I bare my white incisors,
Then rip open the fresh meat,
So as to prevent a flood,
My tongue laps up the blood
Oozing from the animal,
What a tasty mammal.

I am what I am,
I eat what I eat,
As I sit on my righteous seat,
Permeating, the sun's heat.

Who am I?
Fiercer than fire,
More ferocious than the wind,
Wilder than wild.
I am the *lion king!*

Anastasia Kyriacou (13)
Bentley Wood High School, Stanmore

Pure Hatred

As deep as the heart could preach
It searched day and night
As others have taught and teach
At the end of the tunnel there's always light

My tunnel has no end
There are only curves and bends
I am lost in my own world
You shouldn't have gone there I'm always told

My lonely heart, a lost wanderer
It follows a map which tells no lie
A setting sun it has found yonder
Blazing reds dance in the sky

Colours as rich as blood of the wounded
With each soul denuded
Caught in cages with bars of threat
Screaming, he says, pay my debt

Led by faith with no sense
It gropes for a lifeline
Slashing through fear so dense
Fear and terror's paths entwine

No eyes can seek the truth behind bars
When your eyes are plated in tears of glass
Pain stalks your soul relentlessly
A cure is what you want immediately

A journey with the arts of patience
Watching life walk past
Gaining wisdom in an instance
Day by day this world grows vast

I made a vow too strong to break
It winds around my hands like a snake
It haunts my soul day and night
On my mind, is hands grip tight

There is no end to this cycle
For there was no beginning
Yet it appears to melt like an icicle
The Earth soaking its form unaware of its sinning.

Hajra Aziz (14)
Bentley Wood High School, Stanmore

Dumped In The Dark

No one has to know
What you did.
We'll cover it up,
We'll seal the lid.

What you've done,
The consequences,
They ain't fun.

If you'd just stopped to think,
Oh, you silly child,
We don't live on the brink,
You can't run and hide.

There's nowhere to go.

Your friendships will fail,
Needless to say.
All I care about
Is my latest broken nail.

You are alone now,
You're stupid, low,
You started it, now let it end.

There's nowhere to go.

Abby Butcher (14)
Bentley Wood High School, Stanmore

The Black Sheet

Standing on the ground that she wished would feast on her,
Her hands shaking uncontrollably.
Looking down to the black sheet,
The black sheet that would decide her fate.

She knelt down on her knees,
Cupping her hands, begging for hope from the wells of wisdom.
Calling a prayer, pleading,
Inside, her heart bleeding.

Her brain swimming inside her stomach,
Her tongue trapped to the bottom of her mouth.
She looked upon the woman in green,
To wash her salted wounds clean.

Her gentle, silent touch,
Smoothing the crease of the black sheet.
The time had come,
She slowly lifted the black sheet.
'It's her,' she said,
And with one last breath, she shot herself dead.

Charlotte Cohen (14)
Bentley Wood High School, Stanmore

Hatred

Hatred is as black as the night sky.
Hatred is like the taste of a poisoned apple.
Hatred is like the smell of ash.
Hatred looks like a haunted house.
Hatred sounds like a screeching door.
Hatred feels like a ball of fire inside your heart.

Lava Nozad (12)
Bentley Wood High School, Stanmore

The Lazy Tortoise

I'm trapped in a shell
And I know all is not well
Life is such a drag
I'm old and such a rag
'Oh look, is that a leaf over there?'
All I can do is look and stare!

All I do is sit under a willow tree
Hoping one to break free
It's such a struggle to move
But one day I hope to groove.

I do nothing because I'm *soooooo* lazy
And I know it's totally crazy
I'm sitting here trapped in this shell
And it is such a living hell.

Maybe one day I will be able to run free
Because that is how I would like to be!

Kezia Eniang (13)
Bentley Wood High School, Stanmore

He Is Behind You

He lurks in the shadows with a snarl on his face
Waiting for you to slow your pace
You walk with no care, as you think he's not there
Look out, he is behind you.

He lingers in the darkness waiting to strike
For the next delectable child riding her bike
She rides with no care, as she thinks he's not there
Look out, he is behind you.

His bright yellow eyes are the only thing you'll see
That's the only warning before you can flee
You run with care, as you know he is there
Look out, he is behind you.

Nicola Forman (13)
Bentley Wood High School, Stanmore

The Mouse Family

On Monday morning the mice are washing,
It is a very busy day,
Some socks, some shirts, some dungarees,
There is no time for play.

Out digging on a Tuesday,
The mice are clearing weeds,
There is plenty of work to do,
Before they plant their seeds.

On Wednesday the mice are baking,
Crisp cookies fill the tray,
Don and Archie help themselves,
So they are sent away.

On Thursday the mice go shopping,
To buy some tasty cheese,
They also buy some fruit and nuts,
Some carrots and some peas.

On Friday the mice are cleaning,
Each mouse has work to do,
Sweeping, dusting and polishing,
There's so much to get through.

On Saturday the mice decide,
The would like to have some fun,
They all go swimming in the lake,
Then dry out in the sun.

Going jogging on Sunday,
Is what the mice like best,
But Don and Archie run too fast,
And have to stop to rest.

The mice are sleeping in their beds,
It's very late at night,
And outside in the sky above,
The moon is shining bright.

Afifa Khan (14)
Bentley Wood High School, Stanmore

Are You Scared?

Are you scared?
What makes you scared?

The misty dark night
The silence of the gloomy streets
The screech of a little girl
The cry of a dying animal . . .?

What makes you scared?

Admitting to something
Showing your feelings
The slam of a door
The cackle of an evil witch
The laughter in the background . . .?

Are you scared?

The anonymous footsteps
A different taste in your mouth
The first steps into a new world
The noises in the attic
The last drops of water
The last crumb of food
The scratching on a board
The pressure of a gun
The touch of a bullet . . .?

Your last breath?

Are you scared? Am I scared?

Muneerah Yate (12)
Bentley Wood High School, Stanmore

Love

Love is an emotion,
You can feel it in your heart.
I want you to know
I've loved you from the start.

Every day we go to meet,
As if it makes us
Both complete.
I've loved you from the start.

When you're around
I'm not able to speak.
My heart goes thud.
I've loved you from the start.

Now I am writing you this,
To let you know,
Of the sheer bliss.
I've loved you from the start.

Myra Khan (14)
Bentley Wood High School, Stanmore

My Love

My love is like a pin that struck my finger,
My love is like an exotic red rose
or the plumpest red lips.

My love will hold me when I cry,
My love appears like a rainbow after rain,
My love is like springtime when the flowers grow.

My love is blind
I tell no one.

Claire Belfield (12)
Bentley Wood High School, Stanmore

The Lion In The Jungle

I sit and wait
For as long as it takes
For my prey to walk by
To slither or fly

When he finally comes
I jump up and run
With my prey in my mouth
I start heading south

'Til I reach my cave
Where I hide and I save
My dinner for tonight
I can chew with my might

'Til there's nothing remaining
But bones and flesh
I can go back north
For something fresh

I growl and I growl
'Til my hunger goes away
Then my prey comes along
And I chew, chew away.

Nazia Khan (14)
Bentley Wood High School, Stanmore

Happiness

Happiness is like all the colours of a rainbow
It tastes like the bursting flavour of Mentos
Happiness smells like freshly made toast in the morning
It looks like a smiling newborn baby
Happiness sounds like a bird singing sweetly
It feels like a warm summer day on a beach.

Chanté Timothy (13)
Bentley Wood High School, Stanmore

The Calf

I hope I don't die
Here I am in this small wooden box
Bound up with chains and locks.
I hope I don't die.

Stuck here through wind and cold
Hearing others being sold
Wishing, praying, hoping.
I hope I don't die.

I hope I don't die
Here in this small wooden box
I was taken from my mother
She had warm milk and a moo
I wonder if she knows I am here
I really miss her.
I hope I don't die.

I hope I don't die
Here I am in a small wooden box
Bound up with chains and locks.
I hope I don't die.

Frishta Malek (14)
Bentley Wood High School, Stanmore

Fear

Fear is as black as the darkest night
It tastes as sour as the coldest look
Fear smells like the dust in an unwanted room
It looks as though it has been twisted with sadness
Fear sounds like the angry voice of a moody father
It feels as rough as a rock face.

Ebiye Beedie (13)
Bentley Wood High School, Stanmore

Why Me?

In my mind a thing nags me,
and stabs me.
The thing is why do people care
for what I wear?
It's just a piece of cloth, that just hides my
hair and neck.
Does it do any harm? No.
So why do some people
sit and stare?
And when you pass a smile,
they give you a glare.

People may think I sit there,
and judge me with a glare,
also they may think that I don't have any feelings,
but I do.
I do have feelings and I care what you think.
You may think I'm oppressed,
although I'm not.
The scarf is my
dignity, integrity and modesty.
But you rob me of my liberty.

As soon as I put on my scarf there is a knight in shining armour,
shielding me.
I am guarded and protected
like a pearl in an oyster, away
from its thief.

Questions and more questions.
These race in my mind and chase me.
Why can't you accept me
and let me be
who I want to be?

Anam Toufiq (14)
Bentley Wood High School, Stanmore

Imagine If It Happened To You

Try to imagine being bullied
Scared to go out
Scared to have fun, scream and shout
Being the kid who has no friends
Who walks alone, scared to read the messages on their phone
Bullying is not a nice thing to do
Imagine if it happened to you

Crying at night, keeping completely out of sight
Bruises and cuts still mark them
How can anyone be so mean?
Some even very keen
To hurt someone they barely know
Bullying is not a nice thing to do
Imagine if it happened to you.

Tia Wharton (12)
Budehaven Community School, Bude

Teenager In Love

He brightens my day up
and I love him
He has a glint in his eye
and I love him

His teeth shine like diamonds
and I love him
He makes me smile and I go giddy
I do so love him.

Zara Andrews (13)
Budehaven Community School, Bude

So This Is Me

So this is me,
It's time to face the world.
So this is me,
Will my voice ever be heard?
So this is me,
Deformed, disfigured, this is the truth.
So this is me,
I thought my life was accident-proof.
So this is me,
Will people accept me for who I am?
So this is me,
Or will people hate me and not give a damn?
So this is me,
Tears streaming down my face.
So this is me,
My face has now lost its beauty and grace.
So this is me,
It's time to face the world.
So this is me,
Will my voice ever be heard?

Alex Parker (13)
Budehaven Community School, Bude

My Guinea Pig

If I could turn back time,
I would put them in separate hutches,
My rabbit and my guinea pig,
Because they fought.
Every time they met a war would break out,
Eventually one had to go.

My guinea pig died.
I buried him in the garden.

Jamie Shurety-Thompson (13)
Budehaven Community School, Bude

Would You Change War

Bang! goes the English army
Germany shoots back at them
Hundreds of men fall to the ground
As the air is filled with gunpowder

As the English test bomber planes
Germany responds with well armoured tanks
Hundreds of men fall to the ground
As the air is filled with gunpowder

Planes shoot everyone
Not a soul left standing
Hundreds of men fall to the ground
As the air is filled with gunpowder

Only pigs want war
There are no winners, just a death sentence
Hundreds of men fall to the ground
As the air is filled with gunpowder.

Tony Marshall (12)
Budehaven Community School, Bude

Tears In The Snow

Glistening sun on white, rolling snow,
People swaying to and fro,
Skis cutting in, fully controlled.

Then someone shoots by,
You fall, eyes to the sky.
Fear gripping, clinging, not letting go,
You're rolling, rolling through the snow.

Lost in a world
Of white, so cold.
Staggering up and letting go
Of adrenaline, pain that starts to slow.
Then come tears, tears in the snow.

Alex Ward (13)
Budehaven Community School, Bude

An African

It's hot
with dry ground
I am hungry
but haven't got any money
walking for miles just for water
but it saves my life.

I am all alone
with no family to hold me tight
I don't go to school
I haven't had any education
I am scared
I don't know what to do
I wish that I had a family
I feel like no one loves me.

Jordan De Rosa (12)
Budehaven Community School, Bude

The Youth Of Today

The colour of your skin
Does it matter?
No.
It is who you are inside.
ASBOs meant for the gangs,
to help prevent crime and racism.
War, is it worth the loss of life?
Creates upset and tragedy,
also poverty in some countries.

Is this the youth of today?

Teri Jasper (13)
Budehaven Community School, Bude

The Girl Who Cannot Speak

Darkness is all around me,
I cannot breathe.
There are so many people around me.
Yet I am all alone.
I scream and shout, but no one hears me.
The girl who cannot speak.

Even when it's light,
It still gets dark.
The room is so big,
It seems so small.
I'm here but no one sees me.
The girl that cannot speak.

The things I do are right,
They feel wrong to me.
When I talk I hear it,
But nothing comes out.
The girl who cannot speak.
But no one cares,
No one cares about it.

Emily Smith (13)
Budehaven Community School, Bude

The Wild Is A Big, Big Place

The wild is a big, big place
Where animals run at their natural pace
The lions do their roar
Which the elephants think is such a bore
The rhinos charge about
And all the tigers do is shout, shout, shout
The vultures in the sky
The giraffes reaching high
When you see a tree
You'll be sure to hear a chimpanzee.

Peter Copplestone (11)
Budehaven Community School, Bude

Eyes Of A Child

I love the big kids
They know everything
But sometimes they get nasty
Push me from the fun

Sometimes they like me
Sometimes they don't
Sometimes they act like my god

I wish I was big
So they would take notice
I could hang round with them
And play dog eat dog

Sometimes they like me
Sometimes they don't
Sometime they act like my god

Now I am big
I want to be small
Not a care in the world
Not a trouble at all

Sometimes they like me
Sometimes they don't
Sometimes they act like my god.

Georgina Hobbs (13)
Budehaven Community School, Bude

Turn Back Time

Turn back time to when she was
short, young and intelligent.
She was the one that
everyone made fun of.
The one that now is loved by all.
Once she was a cocoon,
now she is a beautiful butterfly.

Cassie Bellinger (12)
Budehaven Community School, Bude

Does Anyone Know Me

I'm standing here, shouting out for help,
Nobody seems to listen,
I've spent all my life in the dark,
I know I need help.

People look at me and presume such nasty things.
Outside I might look confident,
Inside I'm screaming,
Digging myself a bigger hole I can't get out of.

I've always wanted to be someone else,
If I just went,
Would anyone care?
Would I be remembered as
A good girl
A depressed girl or a lonely girl?

I've always wanted to sit in a dark corner,
Try and forget the hurt,
Forget the pain
So many people have caused me.

People treat me like a child,
It's OK to use me.
I cry myself to sleep,
I've run out of luck.

Aimèe Sheridan (13)
Budehaven Community School, Bude

Why?

Life is unfair, nothing is ever right,
I think about it every single second of my life.
When I try to untangle it,
It always bounces back,
But it's like a rubber band with no answers.
Every time it comes to an end,
And still no answers.

Kate Watts (11)
Budehaven Community School, Bude

The Mystery Of A Child's World

Hello there, what's your name?
I'm so glad that you came.
Where am I? What are you?
I really need to go to the loo!

I'm a bee, what are you?
Are you very lost too?
What is this place, right here?
I think I might just shed a tear.

I'm a child, can't you guess?
I wish I wasn't in this mess.
I am lost, yes I am,
I am looking for my nan.

I need to look for my nan,
So I'm going, yes I am.
Hope that I see you soon,
I must go before the moon.

Kieran Gooding (12)
Budehaven Community School, Bude

In Time

If I was to go back in time
I'd change war, I'd change crime
I would stop World War II
I would stop World War I
I would stop it before it began
Peace was right, it's wrong to fight
But people do it every day
And with lives we have to pay
It's not fear anymore
Now just leave it, walk out the door!

Bob Rush (12)
Budehaven Community School, Bude

The World Once Was . . .

The world was whole
The world was pure
The world was undivided
The world was calm

The eagles fly in grace
The fishes swim openly
The trees smile in heat
The people free

The world was whole
The world was pure
The world was undivided
The world was calm

The falcons protect the skies
The sharks command the seas
The lion rules the land
The people free

The world was whole
The world was pure
The world was undivided
The world was calm

This what the world once was

The world is broken
The world is dark
The world is divided
The world is raging

The eagles fall from grace
The fishes struggle in vain
The trees burn in fires
The people drunk and mad

The world is broken
The world is dark
The world is divided
The world is raging

The falcons' blood sheds the skies
The sharks' tears stop the sea
The lions' secret lies buried
The people are in power now

The world is broken
The world is dark
The world is divided
The world is raging

The end of the world will come.

Patrick Zhang (13)
Budehaven Community School, Bude

My Granny

My granny is a nanny,
She is sixty-two,
She lives on a farm with cows that moo.

My granny likes shopping,
But she does not like mopping,
My granny is active but she does not like hopping.

My granny is smart,
She has a big heart,
But she doesn't have a racing cart.

My granny has a husband,
She thinks the world of him,
And she also has a friend called Kim.

My granny has three daughters,
One of which is my mummy,
I love my mummy and my granny.

Lisa Bellairs (11)
Budehaven Community School, Bude

Through The Eyes Of A World War II Soldier

I got the dreaded letter today; it said I was to go to war.
I've got to go to be a man. to prove I'm not a coward.
To leave the wife is the hardest thing.
But what's the point in questioning?
Hitler is not going to win!
I've got to serve my country.

I'm on the truck to go to war,
I've got a picture of my wife to keep on those lonely nights.

I'm in the trench now; we've been here for over two weeks,
Death is around every corner.
Not only the smell is so bad, everyone's eyes are sunken.
All I can think about is home, my wife's warm embrace.

My mind must have wandered somewhere else,
Now we're going to battle, fear so gripping,
My life flashes before my eyes.
Am I going to live? What will happen to my family?

Bang!
The first shot goes,
Bang! bang! bang!
I'm too much of a coward, I run back to the trench
And leave all those men.
I turn the corner of the trench -
A German. His gun pointed directly at me.
I know I'm going to die, but the only thought
I can think of is why didn't I stay and fight?
Either way I'm going to die, but if I'd stayed up on battle,
I would die a brave man, instead, I die a coward.

Katie Bryant (12)
Budehaven Community School, Bude

The Soldier Who Couldn't Speak

I'm a simple man,
I wanted a peaceful life,
I never thought it would turn out this way.
But now I'm dressed in green,
So as not to be seen by the watchful enemy's eye.
There goes the whistle that will gamble my life,
And all who surround me too.
In this dirt-filled trench
There is the terrible stench of death and decay.
So we march over the top.
There is nothing I can do to make this stop,
This suicide mission we embark on.
Their guns fire up,
And we pray to the Lord,
Please spare my life this time.
My friends start to fall,
I can take this no more.
I let my body be filled with lead,
And as I fall to the ground,
I think to myself,
This is my eternal bed.

Jim Morgan (12)
Budehaven Community School, Bude

Under Threat

We trek across the dusty African plains,
This is where they wait.
They hunt us down
As if we were their prey.
After our tusks, our skin,
Then they'll wear us round their neck
Or on their shoulders,
And eat with us,
Like they didn't even kill us.

Rebecca Drew (13)
Budehaven Community School, Bude

A Bird's Eye View Of Suffering

Flying on the sea wind,
Flying through the air,
Why do people hate us so?
Why do they never care?

A young fox I see,
Running for his life,
The hounds are on him now,
Each tooth is like a knife.

Flying on the sea wind,
Flying through the air,
Why do people hate us so?
Why do they never care?

I swoop down to a lab,
A cat I see, screaming and crying,
Wishing she were free,
Now she is broken and is no longer trying.

Flying on the sea wind,
Flying through the air,
Why do people hate us so?
Why do they never care?

On to a farm now,
Gaunt chickens, robbed of dignity,
Staring eyes, featherless wings,
Some of them can hardly see.

Flying on the sea wind,
Flying through the air,
Why do people hate us so?
Why do they never care?

Gwendolen Farrell (12)
Budehaven Community School, Bude

Name

In a world of order
For those unknown, the sorer
Side of life
Joy and strife

No name, whose shame?

A young girl from mid-Asia
Could so easily be
A non-existent image
To catalogued society

No name, whose shame?

If you perceive the rose
As greater than the daisy
Is it the soil or the owner's care
That made it that way?

No name, whose shame?

The sky has not a boundary
The bird is not an immigrant
We share the air so why
A little harder can't we try?

For she is there
Identity true
She needs a name
That's for us to do.

Emma Thomas (13)
Budehaven Community School, Bude

Such A Big World

My mum always tells me I am her big boy
Everything and everyone is bigger than me

As I sit in the yellow, mellow meadows
Birds singing, almost as big as me
Flapping their fluffy feathers, crowding me

Playing on the golden, glazed sand
I squirm in my uncomfy nappy
The roaring white-horsed sea
Coming to get me

When I am not adventuring in my mum's monster beast
Round the country
I will be eating
My food is bigger than me.

Lottie Davies (12)
Budehaven Community School, Bude

Good Times

It's fantastic, nothing but sunshine, it's beautiful
The beach is soft and so warm and tender
It's amazing, everybody is so friendly
I can't wait, it's going to be so fun
The people are like animals in the high street
The bumps on the floor go in a rhythm
My hotel is as tall as a mountain.

Joshua Ravenscoft (12)
Budehaven Community School, Bude

Through A Homeless Person's Eyes

One day my parents had a row,
It kept going on and on,
I wanted it to stop,
So I thought the best way out of it was to run away.

When they had gone to bed and were fast asleep,
I escaped out of my window,
And ran down the street,
I didn't know what to do with myself,
And this is how I became homeless.

I feel really lonely, like no one wants me,
I just want to find a nice clean home,
I try to stop people in cars to pick me up,
But they keep going past.
I don't blame them!

Lloyd Moore (13)
Budehaven Community School, Bude

Nobody

Darkness stirs within me
I'm drawing closer and closer to insanity
I try to speak but nobody listens
Nobody ever listens
Nobody ever cares
I feel like nobody
I'm standing above the sea on a moonlit night
The stars twinkle as I wonder whether to end it
I step closer to the edge and fall over
Down and down into darkness
Now I am truly nobody.

Shaun Wheatley (11)
Budehaven Community School, Bude

My Nan

I have a nan, a special nan.
She's like a blazing fire upon a gentle drop of snow, slowly melting.
She's like a red dragon ready to take flight to the clear blue sky.
She's like the stars and the moon glistening in the darkness.
She's a long-lost island that time forgot.
She's a small kitten waiting for her milk.
She's a lost puppy all on her own.
I have a nan, a special nan.
She's an aeroplane gliding through the dark blue sky.
She's the breath of a human.
She's a dolphin swimming to the deepest depths of the sea.
She's a deep blue pool of light.
Guess what?
She's my nan.

Katie Cunningham (12)
Budehaven Community School, Bude

Nobody's Perfect

School is never kind
They say kids are the harshest race of all

I wear eyeliner, I'm suddenly hard-core punk
I listen to rap, I'm behind a tree, puffin' on a fag
I wear black, beware, I might turn into a bat and suck your blood
I get interested in boys and I'm a slag
Everything we do gets judged and misread

But nobody is perfect
If nobody is perfect
I am nobody.

Beth Wilde (13)
Budehaven Community School, Bude

My Uncle Jon

My uncle Jon is in the marines
And in the war he is never seen
Jon is a sniper
He could shoot down a viper

He is also a medic
For which he should take credit
He's a great uncle, that's for sure
I wish he could be at home more

He's great to spend time with
When he's on leave
An uncle like him
You wouldn't believe!

Chris Merrifield (12)
Budehaven Community School, Bude

The Diary Of A Heart Attack

As I stood there,
I realised they were screaming for me,
As I stood there,
All the butterflies in my stomach
Seemed worthwhile,
As I stood there
They all screamed my name,
As I stood there,
It all went black,
As I lay there,
I had a heart attack.

Tasha Bate (13)
Budehaven Community School, Bude

If The Pen Is Mightier Than The Sword

If the pen is mightier than the sword,
Then the brain should be mightier than the body.

If one has the strength of an ox,
Are they still allowed to cry?

Can someone with the eyes of an eagle
Be blind to the rest of the world?

Some people who can run like the wind
Still must hide.

If beauty is in the eye of the beholder,
What it is no one will behold?

If the pen is mightier than the sword,
Then the brain should be mightier than the body.

Shannon Miller (13)
Budehaven Community School, Bude

Time

If I could turn back time,
I could make everything right.
Like stopping the Blitz by being a spy.
And helping others in Africa before they die.
I could take clothes and food and more from my time
And bring it back to earlier times.
While the moon glistens in the sky
I look down at the sandy floor
And watch the crabs walking by.
I give a person who is sitting next to me some bread.
I am still back in time.

Danielle Smith (12)
Budehaven Community School, Bude

Back In Time

If I could go back in time this is what I'd change:

A blue sun
A yellow sky
Is what I'd change

Green flowers
And purple leaves
This is how it would be

Annoyed, jolly
Argumentative, happy
My life would be great

This is how the world would be.

Eleanor Perkin (12)
Budehaven Community School, Bude

My Dog!

Playing in the garden
Throwing sticks on the beach
Running in the house
Knocking over vases
Getting mud on the carpet
Mum scrubbing your coat

You would chase me up and down the stairs
Never tiring

I'll remember you forever!
You've got a place in my heart.

Matthew Cole (12)
Budehaven Community School, Bude

Through The Eyes Of A Skydiver

8.15 - gravel crunches
The car pulls up at the sky-dive zone
I walk over to the plane
Ready to take off!

9.30 - I'm ready to jump
Feeling anxious but excited
3, 2, 1 - I'm off!
Not falling, but soaring with the help of a wing suit.

I fly off
Fields and cars below look like ants
It's all like a jigsaw!
I feel like a bird in the sky

I pull my chute
I come in to land - *success!*
I land
All I have to do is re-pack my chute
Off I go again!

Alex Butler (12)
Budehaven Community School, Bude

Untitled

I remember you
It was a dark night
Your eyes were dark as the black sky
But at the same time
White as the shimmering snow
I could feel your heavy breath, your fear
I couldn't stand you dying in my helpless arms
But to me you're alive
You're here.

Jenny Persson (12)
Budehaven Community School, Bude

My Brilliant Past

The brilliant times,
All the memories,
Playing together,
Everyone friends.

The brilliant times,
I've left behind,
But then it happened,
I knew my life would change.

The brilliant times,
That I grew out of,
Growing up,
And becoming an adult.

The brilliant times,
When I was young,
Now that I'm older,
I can't cope.

The brilliant times,
The brilliant memories,
My horrible future,
My brilliant past.

Megan O'Neil (12)
Budehaven Community School, Bude

The Time Machine

And into the time machine I leapt
It lifted up and flew away
Time flashed before my eyes
I flew up high
I flew down low
Into the past I went
Flying past trees
Ducking under bridges
The doorbell rang
I was out of the past and into the present.

Kieran Miles (11)
Budehaven Community School, Bude

Fox Voice

We don't mean any harm,
It's not a deadly sin,
We're only on their premises
For one measly chicken.

What is the problem with them?
Why should they care?
Why do they shoot at us?
Surely that's not fair?

Foxhunters everywhere,
Not a place to stay,
Whatever we do
We have to pay.

Our lives are precious,
Not a piece of dirt,
But no, they don't listen,
And we're the ones hurt.

They toss us aside like filth,
They think they know it all,
With their guns and hounds,
Fox heads against the wall.

Our kind is near extinction,
One by one we go,
One by one they pick us off,
This behaviour is so low.

Can we ask one thing?
This request may be my last,
Please help us to fight them off,
We are dying fast.

Garrick Hill (12)
Budehaven Community School, Bude

The Bully

I tease her and I laugh at her,
I tell her how she looks so bad,
But in the end I'm just jealous,
Because my own life is so sad.

They punch me and they kick me,
And they don't give a damn,
My parents are supposed to love me
And make me who I am.

She has no friends now,
She sits all on her own,
She cries just like I want to
But my tears have never shown.

She doesn't dare tell a teacher,
But right down deep inside,
It would be such a relief,
To let out just what I hide.

She is the perfect rich girl
With a loving family,
She has a wonderful mum and dad,
Just the opposite to me.

Sophie Thornton (11)
Budehaven Community School, Bude

The Time Machine

I looked at the great wonder in front of my eyes
Shining, shadowy, still in the moonlight
The time machine - what a beauty with her glittering dials
It was time to travel back in time
As I stepped into the future of time.

Charlotte Shemilt (12)
Budehaven Community School, Bude

Street Life

What was the point?
Scared, nervous
Five nights, five days and food was short
But it would be alright for another few days
The leftover burger, yesterday was good
But when you have to share half with a brother
It's more difficult than you think
The stars in the sky remind me I'm not alone
But the struggle for survival is hard
Frightened and scared
What if she found us? Our mum?
The one who got us into this mess
She always abused us
The thought of going back is dreadful
I need money
My brother's getting hungry and cold
With only one blanket
The thought of where to sleep is on my mind
But if only things were different.

James Kivell (12)
Budehaven Community School, Bude

To My Dog

Good times, good memories
Bring back good memories
Please don't die
We had so many great walks along the cliffs
Every time I was sad, you would comfort me
Please don't die
We've had so many great memories
But now you're going
I know you will be in a better place
You'll see our other pets, bones, go for long walks
We've had great memories.

Nick Feltham (12)
Budehaven Community School, Bude

To Get To The Past

If I could turn back time
I would bomb the plane that flew
Into the Twin Towers.

If I could turn back time
I would play football with Bobby Charlton
And the rest of the England players.

If I could turn back time
I would like to go to 1966
To hold the World Cup.

If I could turn back time
I would meet Glen Hoddle of Spurs
Then go for a tour of Spurs.

If I could turn back time
I would try to save Tupac
From dying, getting shot, just 25.

Jordan Cole (12)
Budehaven Community School, Bude

R1

My engine roaring
My clutch shaking
My acceleration is heart-shaking
Jump on the back, but hold on tight
Nought to sixty at the speed of light
Round the corner, here we go
Oh no! Cop car - now we go slow
Back in the garage for a day or two
Spray me up for a day of fun
Here we go! *Vrum, vrum, vrum, vrum!*

Nathan Parfett (13)
Budehaven Community School, Bude

Look At The World From My Little Cloud

Here I am on my little cloud
The world is so small
And I am so big.

Floating here on my little cloud
Staring at the Earth
Big, green, blue and round.

Down, down, down I go on my little cloud
'Touch down,' I say as I clamber off
The world is so big now, while I am on the ground.

Up, up, up I go on my little cloud
The world is nice and small again
Just how I like it.

I am so big
They are so small
Floating, here on my little cloud.

Tom Morley (11)
Budehaven Community School, Bude

Sunset

As the sea lies peacefully upon the stony shore
The cliff's face leaning over with its weather-beaten bottom
The sun rests in the sky baring only half of its considerably
large radiant glow
Showing above the beautiful horizon
Lower, lower it travels, slowly but surely
Soon the moon will be out
Then darkness
The moon now high in the sky
Replacing the sun.

Jimmy Williams (11)
Budehaven Community School, Bude

When I Was A Child

When I was a child I looked up at monstrous eyes
I walked, I glared
Everybody and everything stared down at me.

I walked into the park and trees boomed down on me
I got lost in mountain-tall grass
I looked up at the grey skies which swallowed me up.

I walked onto the beach
Where the sea pools glistened like diamonds
The sand tripped me up to fall down to the ground
I looked up at the blue skies which swallowed me up!

I flew into the sky
Where the white, fluffy clouds caught my attention
The birds flew past the window
I looked down at the ground which swallowed me up.

Katherine Bryant (11)
Budehaven Community School, Bude

The Bloody War

Blood spraying, fires blazing, a thousand people crying
Guns flashing, cannons smoking, thousands of people dying

What he would do to get out of this pit
But he knew that he would get hit

If he could just go through a door
Away from this bloody war

Go back in time, back in time to the start of this horrid war
Go back in time, back in time to try to stop the war.

Tom Wheeler (13)
Budehaven Community School, Bude

Freedom

Sand, sea, lush green grass.

These are the things I wanted to see,
But I decided to pass,

Because it was here I needed to be.

The first environmental city I lived in,
Drugs, alcohol, smoke all around me,

I felt stuck on a board like a pin,
I always dreamt of sand and sea.

My time had come to escape from here,
My mum and brother both agreed

And so did my dad after he finished his beer,
So we put all our stuff into the car

And left at the first sign of sunrise.

My dad didn't stop at the bar.
I had finally gained my prize . . .

Freedom.

Daniel Thompson (12)
Budehaven Community School, Bude

Good Times

Starry sky glistening in the darkness,
Tree house high up in the branches,
Beach, yellow, sandy, water,
Waves crashing on the shore.

Nicola Payne-Heard (12)
Budehaven Community School, Bude

Soldier In WWII

Distant gunfire
Nervous chatter
Engines rumbling
Smoking cigarettes
Smelling like sweat
I'm going to die
I'm going to die
Sergeant Major shouting
People turning round
Water exploding
Feeling dizzy
Feeling scared
I'm going to die
I'm going to die
Germans shouting in the bunkers
Gate from ship goes down
People loading their guns
Several screams of people dying
People getting wounded
I'm going to die
I'm going to die.

Joshua Sparrow (11)
Budehaven Community School, Bude

Poem

The stars glistening in the dark black sky,
Moonlit sky with silvery flakes of sun,
Blue, light and dark sky dreaming above,
Waving seas racing across the yellow, sparkly sand,
With waves crashing against rocks and cliffs,
Cliffs dark, black and scary, creepy,
The rings shiny and sparkly.

Stacey Thomas (12)
Budehaven Community School, Bude

War

Clip-clop, clip-clop, clip-clop
The sound got slower
And slower
A war horn bellowed
Thousands of clip-clops galloped over the hill
Shouting men chanted, running down the hill
Below, thousands of men facing the enemy
'Spears up!' the general shouted
The spears pointed at the enemy
They engaged in war
War, bloody war
All that was left was blood and weapons
They fought to the death.

Luke Wilson (12)
Budehaven Community School, Bude

Through The Eyes Of A Rabbit

It's just a matter of time
Either dying fast and painlessly
Or dying slowly and painfully
It's my time to die
I could die fast with one perfect shot
The shot of a gun
Or die slowly and painfully from disease
That is coming amongst us rabbits.

I'd prefer the gun.

James Walker (12)
Budehaven Community School, Bude

Life On The Streets

Life on the streets
It's hard to cope,
Horrible people you meet
There is no hope.
It's cold
She's homeless,
She's also bold
Scared of the loneliness.
Being forced to do things
She's unable to do,
It's the last thing
That should happen to you.

Kristina Beech (12)
Budehaven Community School, Bude

No Life, No Help

The day I found out I had HIV
Worst day of my life
My mum, my dad
And my brother and sister had died
I was the only one left
Now I'm waiting
A ticking time bomb inside me
I have no life, no help
No one to talk to
I have no one, no one at all
Just waiting for the day.

David Sellars (13)
Budehaven Community School, Bude

Are You There?

The meaning of life
No one knows
Time passes by
We were put on Earth
Can you hear me?
Can you see me?
Were we made for fun?
Made for a reason?

I go to bed, think to myself
Can you hear me?
Can you see me?
Made for fun?
Made for a reason?
No one knows.

Tova Persson (12)
Budehaven Community School, Bude

My Nan

Life is not fair
The closest person to me died
Living without her kindness
Not breathing the same air

Seeing that she is not there
How could she leave me?
I'm grieving, in pain
She did not deserve to die

I see her in the distance
The outline of her soul
She is gone now
My nan, an amazing person.

Sian Sycamore (12)
Budehaven Community School, Bude

Great Memories

Horses in a field
Grazing, enjoying the grass
Watching happily.

Me and my sister
Getting on well, quietly
Playing, then fighting.

Me and my cousins
Excited to see each other
No fighting, just play.

Making new, good friends
best, that's what they are like
Enjoying happily.

Amy Osborne (11)
Budehaven Community School, Bude

Good Times

Being on holiday is the best
My mates rock like mad!
Swimming all day in the sea
Easter is here, let's eat
Doing homework all day
My friends look out for me
We fall out but friends are forever
Seeing my dad, what happy days
Beach, cinema, park and all sorts
Wow, what happy days!

Chloe Payton (12)
Budehaven Community School, Bude

Flying

I lengthen my roots in the ground,
I stretch my branches as long as I can,
But although I am taller than the rest
I still can't touch the sky
I can imagine
Proud of our high ceiling,
Watching the birds flying high above,
Can they reach?
Small animals scurry and scuttle,
Around my trunk and roots,
They are content with being underground,
What am I not content in the middle?
I concentrate hard,
And slip my mind into a leaf,
A short life will come but I am prepared,
I float from a branch,
Goodbye.
A gust of wind carries me everywhere,
I am flying.

Rachel Lowson (12)
Budehaven Community School, Bude

Wet Bum!

I looked at Mum when I was small
I spoke, she didn't notice me at all
I went outside through the big wooden door
I looked up and thought I was on the floor
I went inside because I needed a drink
I climbed on the side and I fell down the sink
I was in the sink with a really wet bum
So all I could do was shout out *'Mum!'*

Kieran Parish (12)
Budehaven Community School, Bude

Where Were You When The Daylight Died?

I sit and wait to hear your footsteps
Not a sound coming to my doorstep
I met you years and years ago
But this memory will never go.

As I sit in the cold, winter air
It softly sways through my hair
All these days have left me behind
Who knows what I'll find.

The leaves on the trees are falling down
On the floor and turning brown
The rabbits and mice begin to creep
As the daylight dies and settles to sleep.

Josh Danks (14)
Budehaven Community School, Bude

Small

Lost in a world of voices
Look down, there are feet
Look up, there are giants
Shops and people everywhere
This is only a small part of the world
Confused, scared, where has she gone?
Found her
Happy
We're going home, away from town.

Sally Sluggett (12)
Budehaven Community School, Bude

Good Times, Great Memories

His name is Teddy
A small baby wrapped up in his warm, cream blanket
Sleeping soundly in his warm cot which he calls home.

When I hold him close to me
I stare into his perfect, cute face
It is as though he knows me already
As he smiles and gurgles back to me.

He's my nephew, I couldn't wait for him to be born
It was so exciting waiting
I felt like I would burst
He is here at last and I love him
I wouldn't change him for the world!

Amy-Laura Dixon (11)
Budehaven Community School, Bude

Friendly Memories

My friends look out for me
We spend time with each other
They don't hurt me
So I call them good friends
They stick with you through bad times
And they do not leave you behind
You might fall out with each other
But you know that you still want to be friends
I might be 16 but I have a heart of gold to my friends.

Roxanne Edwards (12)
Budehaven Community School, Bude

African Child

I live in a dirty, dry, barren area,
I walk miles for water but when I get there,
There is no clean water.

With no education, I cannot get a job,
I am treated unfairly,
And rely on help from agencies.

We live with our animals
And everyone is dying from AIDS and malaria,
I have lost friends and family . . .

And now I'm afraid it may be my turn.

Jack Whitfield (12)
Budehaven Community School, Bude

I Wish

I wish I had that one last chance
That chance to say goodbye
You don't know how much I miss you
And now you're not here, I'll cry
I dreamed about this all before
And hoped it would never happen
But I guess I was wrong
Every night I look at the stars
And make that one special wish
And say to myself, *could I have done something?*

Charlotte Balston (12)
Budehaven Community School, Bude

If Only

It's too late now, it's all over
If I was granted a wish
It would be to change what I did
Fifteen months ago.

She was just one girl
No one to turn to
But when she was sad
It made us happy.

Every day we went to school
And ever day she cried
Nobody saw
So nothing was changed.

And then one day we waited for her
But she didn't come
We just laughed at the time.

But then one day we cried
Just as she had done
And wished we'd never picked on her
In the first place.

For they'd found her in the road . . .
Dead.

Was it an accident?

Cheyenne Hardwick (12)
Budehaven Community School, Bude

Good Times, Great Memories

Time flies by when you're having fun
Playing on the beach in the sun
Making sandcastles in the sand
Eating ice cream on the rocks
What bliss it was.

Kimberley Anstis (12)
Budehaven Community School, Bude

Great Memories

Christmas joy all around
Ripping presents open all day

Easter chocolate, yum, yum!
Tasty! Tasty!

My birthday
My birthday

Going to Wales
And playing on the beach

My friends are the best
They are always there

My first boyfriend
Cute and lovely
But it ended

That's my life
What's yours?

Kim Holloway (12)
Budehaven Community School, Bude

Great Memories - The Beach

Time goes quickly having fun
Days bathing in the sun
Surfing along the high waves
Brilliant sky all day
Sand trickles under my feet
Vanilla ice cream, yum to eat
As the sun settles down
My friends come round to have a play
What a fantastic day!

Katie Domingo (12)
Budehaven Community School, Bude

My Meaning

I lie on my bed
The moon looking down
I think, *who am I?*
Am I even worth a pound?
I am alone in my life
Just me and my thoughts
Will anyone save me
From my deep despair?
If only I was normal
If only I fitted in
My life would be worth something
My life would be great.

I have nobody in my life
Just me and my thoughts
I lie on my bed
The moon looking down
Does anyone care about me?
I don't know my meaning
Am I just here for fun?
I wonder
Am I worth a pound?

Emily Wright (13)
Budehaven Community School, Bude

Portuguese Memories

In Portugal it is sunny and bright
Hot, like fire burning your skin
The sun shines every day
Playing on the beach is such fun
Jumping over the waves
Sunbathing in the boiling sunshine
Hunting in the rock pools
Smiling at the camera
How I wish I was still there!

Skye Davy (12)
Budehaven Community School, Bude

If Only

If only, if only
I could turn back time
To help him
To save him
My dearest friend
If only.

If only, if only
I could turn back time
I would change it
To make everything as it used to be
If only.

If only, if only
I could turn back time
It would be better
I would be happy again
If only.

If only, if only
I could turn back time
We would be together again
Together as one
If only.

Beth Hartley (12)
Budehaven Community School, Bude

Small

I look at the sky
I am so small
The world's so big
We're all ants to all
I feel so vulnerable now
Even the adults are big
But not me
I am so small.

Becky Dawson (13)
Budehaven Community School, Bude

I Can See . . .

I can see my future,
I can see myself passing exams,
I can see myself going to university,
I can see myself falling in love,
I can see myself getting my dream job,
I can see myself having and loving a child,
I can see myself happy,
I can see my future.

I am living my future,
I passed all my exams,
I've been to university,
I am deeply in love,
I've got my dream job,
I'm caring for my precious little child,
I'm as happy as I wished,
I am living my future.

Sammy Pettit (12)
Budehaven Community School, Bude

Looking Into Someone Else's Eyes

Imagine what it would be like to see yourself
In someone else's eyes.
Imagine what it would be like to see
How you really behave and what people think of you.
How would you look? How would you act?
Imagine watching someone waste their life away
Just think what you're about to do before you do it.

Dom Clapton (12)
Budehaven Community School, Bude

If I Could Turn Back Time

If I could turn back time,
I wouldn't be as selfish,
I'd keep my room much tidier
And make my choices much more carefully.

If I could turn back time,
I'd be nicer to my parents,
I'd get along with my sister
And help around the house.

If I could turn back time,
I'd help out more for charity,
I'd raise awareness for missing children
And help to stop animal cruelty.

If I could turn back time,
I'd do things a lot differently.

Lauren Meadows (12)
Budehaven Community School, Bude

Double-O-Nothing

Waiting
Waiting
Listening to voices
Thinking of what will happen next
I'm keeping myself to myself
My heart is beating fast
I'm breathing heavily
Trying not to make a sound
Trying not to move
I'm an unknown presence
I'm the next James Bond
I'm . . . I'm . . . I'm found by Mum.

Courtney Ward (12)
Budehaven Community School, Bude

Do They Even Remember Her Name?

She died,
Two years ago today,
But I was not brave,
She was my best friend,
Until it started.
The bullying began,
I walked away from her,
To join the crowd.
I stood and watched,
They made threats,
But I didn't stop it.
She knew she was going to die.
She wrote a note one night,
It said:
'Mum, Dad, love you lots,
Don't ever forget me!'
Then she left,
Went by the edge of a cliff,
She jumped!
We just looked on.
What if I hadn't walked away from her?
Would it have happened to me
Or not at all?
I should have saved her.
Do they even remember her name?

Shannon Mannix (12)
Budehaven Community School, Bude

Child's Eyes

Aged one, and scared,
Intimidated, clueless,
Unloved or loved?
Switch between the two,
Unable to speak like the others.
Who are they Mummy?
Crying, crying,
Unsure why,
Fuss too much,
Wishing to be older,
To be capable,
Looking up at siblings,
Having fun as I sit here,
With my bottle,
Pretending to sleep.
I have feelings,
Just like them,
But no one understands.
This world is confusing,
Full of giants,
Shouting, screaming,
Help me, Mummy,
I want to get out,
Frightened Mummy, frightened.

Rebecca Piper (12)
Budehaven Community School, Bude

A Look Through His Eyes

I sat on the oozy mud
My head pouring with blood
My arm, my leg, oh, the pain
I had seen a small German plane

An open gash to the head
As all my teammates fled
Bruises, cuts and scrapes, they all bled
No doctor, no stretchers and no bed

The Germans had taken us as they would
Get shot by a gun, a rifle they should
Pull and kick or fight for the world I could
Why did I come? What was the point? Why should I stay?

By the time the gas had gone
When there was a clearance of bombs
I was scalded, broken and burnt, and yet bold
By now I should be dead and it's freezing cold

The rain will pour and a flood will come
The dead bodies swept away
I wish we could make the Germans pay
I close my eyes, the sun will go. My heart stops.

Jade Kirkum (12)
Budehaven Community School, Bude

Youth Of Today

Not every youth is bad,
The police have gone mad,
Am I going to jail?
Will I get released on bail?
I didn't steal anything of the sort,
Will I get punished? Will I get caught?
Even if I'm wearing a hoodie,
I still might be a goody-goody.
Not every youth is bad,
The police have gone mad.

Jack Parratt (12)
Budehaven Community School, Bude

Why The Hell Should I Tidy My Room When The World's In Such A Mess?

I open my window to a cool midnight breeze
Trying to answer a question I've been thinking about for days
But now I think I've found the key
You see I've been trying to look at the world
Through the eyes of a child
Through the eyes of me

My world I thought was a good place
But then it became clear every corner I turned
I found another tear

I also thought it was full of happiness and cheer
But still every corner I turned I found ugly fear

The world is so confusing, as confusing as chess
And then it becomes clear to me
Why the hell should I tidy my room
When the world's in such a mess?

William Middleton (13)
Budehaven Community School, Bude

Poverty

We never think about the people who starve in pain,
Work all day, painful with strain.
Thin and bony, so tired, no fun,
How would you feel without family - no dad, no mum?

If I had the power to help those in need,
I would give all my money until I succeed.
I would change their routine of the day,
Poverty kills, in silence they lay.

I think about those who need our help every day,
The memories of sadness and pain
Will stay with their soul
And never go away.

Coreen Thorne (12)
Budehaven Community School, Bude

Always

We are here
Can they not help us?
Locked inside our minds
Lost and lonely
Despairing forever
Locked inside our minds.

Despair is here
Inevitably here
Can they not help?
Why?

Always here
Lost forever
Can't find us
Help us, help
Never find us
Lost for all eternity
Darkness surrounds us
Help, help.

Closing chasm
We are in
Cannot get out
They could help
Always there
Always, for eternity.

They are coming
I see them coming
Through the eternal gloom
No, they've fallen
Down, down.

Always here
We are here
Can they not help?
Always waiting
We are here
Locked inside our minds.

Caitlin Quinn (12)
Budehaven Community School, Bude

War, War, War

War is bad and no one likes it
But all the time it happens
I don't think we can ever stop it
It just keeps happening
And more lives are lost
I want it to stop
Stop right now
But what can I do?
I'm only a child
No one will listen to my point of view
Every second lots of lives are lost
Too many people die
But all the time these things happen
And never can be stopped
Why does it happen to us?
I don't know why
I want it to stop
And never happen again.

Jake Cartwright (13)
Budehaven Community School, Bude

My Life - Whose Life?

A flash of colour
A speck of noise
I stay there silent
Paralysed.

The monsters draw near
The Devil himself
I don't know to move
Or to stay on the spot.

I lift up my body
Get ready to run
Because I'll be too late
At the sound of the gun.

When I hear them sniffing
Their claws on the ground
As quick as a flicker
I go and descend.

I think I'm safe
I know I'm not
I run by the hedgerow
Only just out of shot.

I need to cross the field
There is no long grass
My cubs will die
If I'm foolish and get lost.

I have to cross the field
There is only short grass
My cubs will die
If I'm not brave, and cross.

I crouch down low
I get ready to go
I run like the wind
Until I hear gunshots.

It follows me swiftly
I have to keep running
It has less chance of hitting me
There in the bushes.

I'm afraid I'm not lucky
I'm afraid I have lost
Lost the grand battle
Lost my heart, and my cubs.

Holly Smale (12)
Budehaven Community School, Bude

Turn Back Time

If I were to turn back time
The world would be sublime
It would be better if there was no war
Most of it is just a bore

Why don't people get to belong?
Why don't people get along?
At the end of the day we're all the same
Why do some of us get the blame?

Animals live their own path
They get all the aftermath
Forests are being chopped down
People think they wear the crown

If there were no pollution
Is there no solution?
If I were to turn back time
The world would be sublime.

Matt Eusden (12)
Budehaven Community School, Bude

That Bloody Tree!

That tree ruined my holiday,
It felt like years, it felt like days.

But landed now, something cracked,
That day my life was just snapped.

All my body was in shock,
I felt I was under key and lock.

I'd broken my arm in two different places,
They crowded around, lots of blank faces.

A metal plate was encased,
In my arm it will stay.

Just to come out,
Another day.

Barnaby Simpson (13)
Budehaven Community School, Bude

Turn Back Time

If I could turn back time
I would play for Man U, in 1999
And I would pick up the Champions League
And Premiership trophy
And the FA Cup.

If I could turn back time
I would be the ref in the World Cup final
When England played Argentina
When Maradona made that hand-ball
I would disallow it and England would still have a chance.

Jordan Davis (13)
Budehaven Community School, Bude

Abandoned

Lonely and abandoned
Longing for a place like home
No one to comfort
No one to hold

Just sitting here abandoned
No one to fend off my fears
I seem to be invisible
As no one notices my tears

Looking all around me
Everyone so big
All of them are giants
Whereas I'm just a kid.

Lauren Miller (12)
Budehaven Community School, Bude

Through The Eyes Of A Child

I walk through a door
The size of a house
Terrified and small
To see giants smiling at me
Hugging and holding me for evermore

But now I am older
Almost as tall as that door
So now when I see little toddlers
I know what they're thinking
They're thinking about that door.

Matthew Whitefield (13)
Budehaven Community School, Bude

The Elephant Song

Huge feet as big as boulders,
Colossal trunk giving off sound,
Elephant, I heard you
Roaring.

Instead of your life we choose,
Keys for our keyboards,
Ornaments for our mantels.

Great mountain in Africa,
Living with your friends,
Elephant, I heard you
Playing.

Instead of your life we choose,
Keys for our keyboards,
Ornaments for our mantels.

Elephant, if humans didn't poach,
Your memory would be enormous,
You're forever remembering.

Instead of your life we choose,
Keys for our keyboards,
Ornaments for our mantels. Why?

Sophie Jenks (12)
Budehaven Community School, Bude

Through A Victim's Eyes

You may think I am happy
But inside myself I'm sad
Sad about what's happening to me
Things disgraceful and bad

I've always been a nice girl
Never put a foot out of place
Now I'm sitting here on my own
With a sad look on my face

I have no friends of my own
They're all too scared to know me
They do not like the way I am
But in the end, that's all I can be

They turn my friends against me
Talk behind my back
I want to just stand up to them
But courage is one thing I lack

I really try to hold my tears
But they just run down my face
I'm the invisible girl in the 'big, bad world'
Lost and out of place.

Sophie English
Budehaven Community School, Bude

Child Abuse

As I slowly awake, Mummy comes up to find me still in bed.
She freaks. Grabbing an old belt, she beats me.
It hurts. I want to cry, but I hold the tears back.
I long for her to love me. Why doesn't she?
I love my mummy, why doesn't Mummy love me?

I go to school, I mask what really happens in my life.
I hide the pain and sorrow.
Hiding the bruises, I put on a fake smile.
Today in class we had to write about our parents.
Many of my friends picked their mummy.
I love Mummy, why doesn't Mummy love me?

People have their suspicions about my life.
I don't know my daddy, Mummy says he is evil.
She says if I'm not careful I'll grow up to be just like him.
I love Mummy, why doesn't Mummy love me?

I cry, I get bullied at school because I don't wear the right clothes,
Or I'm too skinny, or smell funny.
Mummy makes me wear clothes for days on end.
I love Mummy, why doesn't Mummy love me?

My teacher came and asked me if I was OK, she saw the bruises . . .
'How did you get them,' she asked.
'I fell,' I said.
I had no one to write about.
I don't know my daddy and my mummy doesn't love me.
I love Mummy, why doesn't Mummy love me?

Making my way home from school,
People stare and grumble at me, I wonder why.
I make my way through my front door,
Mummy is waiting for me on the stairs.
I'm scared.

I see the belt behind her back and I run to the kitchen.
She follows me.
What am I to do?
She beats me.
I scream and fall to the floor.
I love Mummy, why doesn't Mummy love me?

Briony Smith (12)
Budehaven Community School, Bude

Untitled

Alone she stands,
The cuts just below her hands.

They say she's ugly, stupid and weak
I mean, look at the worthless little freak!

They go one step further today
Whisper, 'One more order to obey.'

The boy watches closely from the corner
But no way has he got the guts to warn her.

A kick in the teeth, her eyes start to pour
As she suffers in silence, blood drips to the floor.

Off home she goes, straight up the stairs
And thinks to herself, *why bother? Nobody cares.*

Two doors away, the boy senses something wrong
A feeling that has never been quite so strong.

The mother's one and only daughter
Slowly lowers her head into the water.

Over he goes, the door is unlocked
Makes his way in and finds himself shocked.

A note he finds left on the mirror
'They put me through hell and now Heaven is nearer.'

With his body and soul, her spirit remains
And the rest of him . . . caught up in chains.

Lola Thorpe (12)
Budehaven Community School, Bude

That Girl

The way that she walks,
The way that she talks,
It's enough to drive anybody insane,
It's like she looks through the pain.

The pain she caused,
It was like she made my life pause,
She took the one thing I had,
Now everything is so bad.

I want to shout out loud,
I would if there wasn't such a crowd,
They try to gang up on me,
They act as if I am three.

But I will not stand alone,
As if I am a queen sitting on my throne!
She won't do this to others,
Because we will stick together like brothers.

I won't be looked down on,
Because this is one big con,
I won't let these tears roll down my face,
Because I am not a disgrace.

Francesca Metherell (11)
Budehaven Community School, Bude

Magical Rose

This is the touch of a unicorn's hair
This is the evil of Lucifer's lair
This is the sunlight that filters through trees
This is the buzzing of hard-working bees
This is the wonder of Shakespeare's words
This is the dreaming of mythical birds
This is the tear of a heartbroken sky
This is a taste of the power of why
This is the feel of the great fairy rings
This is the beat of a butterfly's wings
This is the war of the heart and the mind
This is the treasure of what you will find
This is the aura of something that lives
This is the love of all that nature gives
This is the colour whose name no one knows
This is the essence of magical rose.

Cicely Street-Mellor (13)
Clyst Vale Community College, Exeter

Stupid Like A Cod

'From the Italian to the Spanish waters,
Swim all my seven hundred daughters.'
King Cod was the ruler of all the ocean,
His subjects served him with devotion;
Except for one, the wily shark,
Whose envy made his heart grow dark.
To this, however, King Cod was blind,
Producing an heir obsessed his mind.
True, he had seven hundred daughters,
But his only son had just been slaughtered.
With nobody to take the crown,
The dynasty of Cod would drown.
So the king (with this exhausted mother),
Tried to give the girls a brother.
But even with ten thousand spawn,
The needed heir was never born.
The king called on his fishy court
And unto them his problem brought.
From dolphins to prawn they thrashed about
And tried to sort the problem out.
The shark told the king he'd had a notion,
To track the trawlermen on the ocean,
With a bite of bait on the end of their rod,
He would finally produce an heir to Cod.
The naïve king thought this idea was best,
Immediately starting his foolish quest.
While on this endeavour the king was caught
And the kingdom of Cod became but nought.
The moral of this story, a fishy tale,
Don't be stupid like Cod - you'll surely fail.

Adam Ward (14)
Colyton Grammar School, Colyton

Summer Is . . .

S eas that are as clear as the sky
U sually yachts sail slowly and smoothly
M ums and dads swimming together
M anatees gliding in the sea
E veryone is going on their holidays
R unning across the beach

Little children making sandcastles
Divers swimming with dolphins
Little girls picking flowers in the field
Hungry kids eating ice cream
Mums putting on suncream
Families having picnics on the beach

The sun glistening on the waves
Crabs scuttling into rock pools
Chalk making the sea white
Piles of green seaweed
Shells hidden under sand
Cliffs reaching up to the clouds.

Dominic Williams-Stevens (13)
East Court School For Dyslexia, Ramsgate

Seaside Poem

O ffices are closed
N ice sun shining on me

T he soothing sea
H iring a sailing boat to drive
E njoying quality time with my family

B irds flying in the air
E ating burgers
A way from work and jobs
C ooling drinks and ice cream
H orse riding early in the morning.

Sebastian Wilkins (13)
East Court School For Dyslexia, Ramsgate

Colours Poems

Red:

Red is the colour of many things
Some are good and others bad
It can mean fury, maybe even anger
Or it could mean danger
But it could also mean red noses
Or even a bunch of red roses.

Red is the colour of many things
Some are good and others bad
It could be the colour of blood
Or it could mean to stop
And go no further
This is what I am going to do
And go no further!

Blue:

Blue is the colour of many things
Some are good and others bad
It can mean a cloudless, sunny sky
Or a calm, blue sea
But on a cold winter's day
You can never see this
The sea is frozen over with ice
And the sky is all cloudy
But when the winter is over
And the summer begins
The sky clears up and the ice melts
The cold winter's day is replaced by
A warm summer's day with blue sky and blue sea.

Pink:

Pink is the colour of many things
All are good and none are bad
It could be one day of the year
It is Mother's Day

The one day when mothers are given a rest
They get the day off
No cooking, cleaning, or any of that
They're given a cake and a card
It's the one day of the year
When they're given a break.

Sean Cragg (13)
East Court School For Dyslexia, Ramsgate

Seaside

Summer on the beach is the best thing that can happen to you.
Summer at the beach is a time to enjoy yourself.
You can make sandcastles, have a picnic and an ice cream.

Summer is hot and sticky when you have had ice cream.
Summer is a time for swimming in the lovely sea.
Summer on the beach is having fun and a good time.
Summer on the beach is having a party and a barbecue.

Summer on the beach is sitting on the sand and sunbathing.
Summer on the beach is playing sport on the sand.
Summer on the beach is listening to the birds making noises.
Summer on the beach is for water fights and a good time.

Summer is a time on the beach to see the fish.
Summer on the beach is watching the sun set at night.
Summer on the beach is watching people running around.
Summer is a time to go on a beach and have the time of your life.

Sam Draper (12)
East Court School For Dyslexia, Ramsgate

Seasons

On a winter morning,
Snow tops the hills, like icing on a cake,
Icicles point down like daggers,
Rain patters on the roof like drums banging
And the atmosphere, so brisk and cold.

In spring,
Birds sing like a choir of angels,
Waterfalls surge like a burst pipe,
Fog covers the city like a grey blanket
And flowers bloom so colourful and bright.

During summer,
Fruit ripens like plants flourishing,
Beaches fill like a crowd gathering,
The sun heats the land like a cake baking
And days become longer, whilst nights become shorter.

In autumn,
Trees shed their leaves like confetti falling at a wedding,
Winds blow like flags waving,
The first frosts fall like an Arctic chill
And crops are harvested for winter supplies.

Robyn Lockyer (13)
Exeter School, Exeter

The Mountain Of Peril

Snow topped the mountain like icing on a cake
The moon glowed like a shimmering ocean
The bewildered traveller stumbled and plummeted like a stone
Crashing into ledges as she fell
Screaming her final scream
One of pure terror.

Chris Clay (12)
Exeter School, Exeter

War

The fog covered the ruins like a blanket
The general gave the order to tank it
The grassy dewdrops reflecting the sky
As the tank trails rolled by and by

The rivers flowed full of blood and sorrow
As the soldiers peeped out of their burrows
The water and mud mixed into a mush
As the commander called for a hush

The silence covered meadows all around
Then suddenly a tiny, minute sound
A slight, miniscule whirring
As the generals glanced, concurring

Then suddenly, a catastrophic *boom!*
As Spitfire planes pierced through the gloom
Their machine guns chewing up the den
The sirens signalling the end.

Sam Jellard (12)
Exeter School, Exeter

Mother Nature

The air smelt like new-mown grass
The wind rushed through the house like a tiger
The soft breeze on her face was as gentle as a mouse
Snow topped the mountain like icing on a cake
His stomach rumbled like an earthquake
Snow drifted to the earth like talcum powder
The clouds as fluffy as a cat
Smoke floated on the air like fine silk.

Sam Russell (13)
Exeter School, Exeter

What's Out There?

As I watch the moon like a hungry hawk,
It shimmers like an ocean.

Then snow drifts down like feathers from the sky,
I wish I could see the ocean.

My mother comes and shouts in my ears,
Like an angry bear.

She asks why I'm not in the warm, inside,
I say I don't really care.

Her hair frames her face like a round picture,
She looks all concerned.

'I'd like to cross the ocean,' I say,
'And sail my boat like a whale heading for freedom'
And soon I will be returned.

Alice Tolson (13)
Exeter School, Exeter

A Summer Morn

As I opened my window, I could smell the air
It smelt as fresh as newly cut grass
And the birds were singing in the trees
Like a little girl singing sweetly
I could see the ocean in the distance
It was shimmering like the glowing moon
The sky was so blue
And the clouds were as fluffy as whipped cream.

Emily Kirk (13)
Exeter School, Exeter

The Little Girl

This little girl scuttled across the beach
Like a kitten falling over its feet
Talking to herself as she ran.

In front of her, the rolling hills
With wild flowers dotted over them like polka dots
And roses, their petals as delicate as fairy wings.

The surface of the sea, with ripples, but smooth
The clouds as fluffy as her own cuddly toy
The soft breeze on her face was as gentle as her mother's kiss.

Bryony Mann (13)
Exeter School, Exeter

Life

Outside, the fog covered the city like a blanket,
While the traffic moved as slowly as a snail
And the rose petals were as delicate as glass.
The icicles pointed downwards like stalactites
And the children scuttled across the beach like hermit crabs.
The wind rushed through the house like a hurricane,
With snow drifting down to earth like a deflated balloon.

Tom Pearson (13)
Exeter School, Exeter

Wondrous Winter

In the morn, noon or night
The air smelled as fresh as a moorland day
Snow drifted to the earth like petals blown on the wind

Dewdrops glistened on the flowers like crystal tears
Smoke floated on the air like blackbirds on a summer breeze
In the morn, noon or night.

Cameron Starling (13)
Exeter School, Exeter

Seasons Poem

When pansies are purple
Flowers are ripe
The leaves on roses are spread
But in the gloomy winter
They lie cold and dead

In autumn trees are bare
Their leaves remain below
Friends walking past
They wave and smile hello

Summer is the time for lilies
With beautiful petals that burn
And on the hedge are
Rows of hot, green ferns

Spring, summer, autumn, winter
All are seasons that are fun
Everyone happy
Me, my sister, Dad and Mum.

Charlotte Fanson (12)
Great Torrington School, Torrington

Calves

Day after day I watch them grow
As I will for years to come,
It's a daily job that I love.
I love the thought of waking up early in the morn,
They shout and shout for their milk!
They're my life
And I don't know what I would do without them.
Farming and calves mean the world to me
And they always will.

Dean Folland (12)
Great Torrington School, Torrington

Happy Days

Waterlogged pitches
Mud swept across my face
Bones breaking, bones cracking
And people hurting
Getting stamped on and being munched
Those are the days I adore the most
When I'm getting hurt and scoring tries
There was once a time
I scored a try right in the corner
There was once a time
I stopped a try right under the posts
There was once a time
I could have scored a try
But I dropped the ball over the line
Those are the days I adore most.

Charlie Elliott (11)
Great Torrington School, Torrington

Snow War

It was a cold winter's morning,
The frost had caught me,
Like a sweep of dust,
Coming over my head.
I stepped out,
So far so good,
Now just 100 more
And . . .
Fire!
A snowball hit me,
War had started, many fell.
Now it was just me and him.
What would happen?
No one knew.

Bethany Piper (12)
Great Torrington School, Torrington

Detention

Sitting there waiting
For it to end
Tummy rumbling
Clock ticking

Finishing work
At lunch time
People running
People screaming

In the crammed corridors
Getting their lunch
Detention ends
Food's gone

Cafeteria closed
People laughing
People joking
Bell rings.

Melissa Troke (12)
Great Torrington School, Torrington

Friends

Friends are great
Because . . .
They cheer you up
When you're feeling sad
They stick up for you
If you're being bullied
They never leave you
On your own
They invite you to places
Where you can have great fun
That's why friends are so great!

Ruby Cockwill (12)
Great Torrington School, Torrington

The Boring Old Bus

The bus, the bus
The boring old bus!
The rain against the window
The giggles in the back seats
The songs on the radio
The scraping of wet feet . . .

The bus, the bus
The boring old bus!
My bag weighs a ton
My socks drenched through to my skin
My hair soaked and frizzy
My seat lumpy and rough . . .

The bus, the bus
The boring old bus!
My stop's coming up
Trudging off the bus
Rushing to the door
As the sun comes out . . .

Mollie Gilbert (12)
Great Torrington School, Torrington

Colours

In a shiny box lies brightness,
Darkness and brilliant colours,
Colours of blue, green, purple and red,
Pink and lovely gold, orange, brown,
Black and white,
Colours exploding all over walls,
Exploding like a big balloon
When a needle hits it,
Then a booming *boom!*

Kathy Turner (11)
Great Torrington School, Torrington

Winter's Day

As the snowflakes start to fall,
Twinkling and glistening,
I walk,
The snow's
Crunching and crackling
Under my feet,
I go inside,
As I open the door,
It's like a wave of heat,
Hugging me like a blanket,
The fire is glowing,
Lighting up the whole room,
I look out the window,
Everything is white,
Everything is sparkling,
Trees with no leaves,
Robins are singing,
On this beautiful, wonderful winter's day.

Jess Courtney (12)
Great Torrington School, Torrington

My Life

My life is like one big dream,
I live life to the full,
Having fun and being cool,
That is what life is for.

I have best friends,
Who care all the time,
There's Cerri, Amber and Rikki too,
They make my life worth living,
We are always giggling,
And having laughs,
That is what life is for.

Cally Charles (11)
Great Torrington School, Torrington

Young Writers - Away With Words Poems From The South

The Quarter Pipe

It looms above
I ride over the fun box
It fills my heart with dread
I'm halfway up
Already wanting to quit
What to do?
It's so strange
At the top, balancing on the nose
I lean onto my left arm
The right dangling in the air
An amazing gymnast plant
In a 360 back down
The quarter pipe whizzing past
Thankful for it to be over
The crowd cheering.

Zak Stevens (12)
Great Torrington School, Torrington

Snow Dreams

Cold, gentle evening
Frost crystal-clear
Snow sparkling white
Soft as a kitten
Cuddling up warm and tight
Burning boiling coal
Sweet smells of delicious crumbling cake
A nice hot, bubbly cup of cocoa
Snow dreams are upon us.

Amy Phillips (11)
Great Torrington School, Torrington

Playtime (At Beaford)

The monkeys have been let out,
Rush hour's just begun,
Put down your books,
Put down your pens,
Come on, have some fun.

Playing here, laughing there,
Rolling down the hills,
Shed's been open,
Footballs out,
Let's go run about.

The bell's rung,
It's time to go,
Stuff back in the shed,
In your lines,
Do not talk,
It's time to use your head.

Gemma Hookway (11)
Great Torrington School, Torrington

Freedom!

Here it is, the big black stallion,
Its fierce-looking eyes,
Like the depths of the ocean,
The whip of its tail,
The freedom of its heart,
The crunching of its teeth as it grazes on the riverbank,
The shaking of its mane as it rears on the hill,
The flashing of its hooves as it starts cantering towards the beach,
The strength of its muscles as it begins galloping along the
                                                sand dunes,
The passion of its whole body.

Danielle Colley (11)
Great Torrington School, Torrington

There's A Monster In My Closet

There's a monster in my closet,
Is it red or green or blue?
It's hiding in my closet,
It's coming to get you!

Is it scaly, bald or slimy?
Just think what it could be,
There's a monster in my closet
And it's trying to get me!

The shadow's getting closer,
It's like a giant rat,
It's going to jump out at me,
Oh my God! It ate my cat!

I can hear the screaming noises
Coming from its belly,
I can hear it scratching on the wall,
Like a blackboard on the telly!

The noise is getting louder,
I need to get my mother,
Then suddenly out it jumps . . .
Oh! it's just my little brother!

Cerri Gaskin (11)
Great Torrington School, Torrington

Motoring Motorbike

My menacing motorbike is fun
It goes *a-vroom, a-vroom*
I love my motorbike and do insane stunts on it
I don't care if I hurt myself and fall off
Jump back on I will.

My motorbike may go wrong
I do miss it when it breaks down
To pay for the petrol I may
It's good fun at the end of the day
Doesn't bother me how much petrol
Prices are going up and down
It doesn't make me frown.

I will have motorbikes for all my years
Bringing my mum to tears
Riding every day of my life
No matter how badly I'm hurt
I'll still ride until I die.

Hayden Simpson (11)
Great Torrington School, Torrington

Hope's Breach

I watch for you,
From my perch of endless ageing,
Hoping that today could be just a second longer.
A second more to spend with you.
When will you come?

The endless waiting turns my hair white,
A dirty, creamy white.
You're not here.
I have watched countless sunsets,
Each boringly beautiful.
I don't know if I can wait anymore, please
Hurry, I'm breaking.

Tomorrow.
You used to say that everything will be better,
When tomorrow's eve falls upon me.
I'm still here, but you're not coming.
You won't answer me.
You won't tell me what's wrong.

The steady beat has faded.
There is no tomorrow.
I won't wait anymore,
I know that you're not coming.
You're gone forever.

Jane Drummond (15)
Holsworthy Community College, Holsworthy

Not In My Eyes

Tough as an old boot on the outside,
But soft and gentle on the in,
Puts on a brave face for all the world to see,
He has grown up through the decades,
With wars, rules and strictness.

He has been brave when his country needed him,
He has been bold, he speaks his mind,
A true man, a lover of sports.

He is labelled as strong,
But I know the real man behind the mask,
The man who secretly wants to hug you
And have a kick about.

A man whose coldness is really an act,
A man whose personality will always shine through,
Whose quick-wittedness has got him
Out of many scrapes,
A man who has made his dreams a reality.

He loves sport,
He loves his family,
He loves time alone, but then don't we all?
He loves to make you laugh,
He hates to see you cry,
He's brave and will always be in my eyes,
Because that's him, my grandpa,
Him behind his hazel eyes.

Natalie Boardman (13)
Hurst Lodge School, Ascot

My Nan

My nan worked all day when she was younger,
She worked her heart and soul into life,
Didn't listen to what people said,
Just worked.

But when she was getting old
It was different,
Her hands didn't work anymore like they used to.
She sat in her seat fiddling with her glasses
And falling asleep . . .

But when she began to talk to me
Her face lit up,
Talking to someone made her happy and relaxed
And looking at me with her bright blue eyes,
Made me realise how lucky I was
To speak to someone who loved me.

The day came . . .
While squeezing my hand and whispering in my ear,
Her soft, crinkly lips suddenly touched mine,
Our last goodbyes . . .

But her looking over me now
Is a gift that only I can see.

Sophie Whitlam (14)
Hurst Lodge School, Ascot

Just An Old Friend

How could one heart
Care for so many others,
And each one
Before her own?

She warmed each heart,
With her warming face,
Her happy smile
And her giving ways.

She gave and gave,
Until all was gone,
She helped out wherever possible,
Even towards the end when she was struggling.

She lived for the future,
Not for the past,
Forever positive in her heart,
But forever was cut short.

I knew the day would come,
But once she became sick,
Her life quickly wilted,
Like a flower touched by frost.

So many things I should have said,
Should have done,
But now my eyes are salty
And sore.

Because she has left us
Before her time,
I had no time to explain
How much I cared.

Rebecca Ayers (13)
Hurst Lodge School, Ascot

My Grandma

Lonely she sits at the window
There is only herself to take care of now
He is gone, her protector and provider

How will she survive without him?
But she must stand straight for her family's sake
Even if she is breaking inside

She grows more tired of living a lie
But she must for her family's sake
Even if the price is too high

The pain is becoming etched into her face
Her wrinkles becoming deeper
He kept her young, but now she knows
She is a very old woman indeed

First her son, now he has left her too
She would not make it through the day
If it weren't for her little weeps every night

The empty place beside her while she tries to sleep
Is a fresh reminder of the pain she bears
And will bear for the rest of her life

All day long she potters about the house
What use is cooking for one person
And she makes little mess, so what to do?

Nothing seems worth it anymore
The love of her life, her husband
Is gone.

Michelle Kruger (13)
Hurst Lodge School, Ascot

Childhood Dream

The river sparkled
With the enchantment of the sun
The golden fish
That flew and glided
A petal floated
As the sun warmed the air

The ivy weaved up the wall
Flowers blossomed
And filled every life
With the scent of hope

A butterfly looped and fluttered
The birds whistled to the breeze
As it cooled the hot summer's day
And your world was filled with dreams

The wind blew and slid
Through fields of green
As life was reborn
Through a childhood dream.

Hayley Weeks (13)
Hurst Lodge School, Ascot

In My Mind

In my mind
He was always old
But if I look back
I remember
When he ran
And played
And sometimes scuttled sideways
After crabs along the beach

But mostly I remember him
Being old and frail
Eventually he got too old to go for walks
And just padded around the house
All day we overlooked him
And it wasn't until he was gone
That I realised
Just what a huge part of my life he was
To me.

Sarah Brown (14)
Hurst Lodge School, Ascot

She

She doesn't know how to say goodbye,
The fear is sweeping over her, she doesn't know why.
She's scared and shaking
And inside her heart is breaking.

She can't understand why she's losing her way,
Her grip is loosening, but she wants to stay.
Her head hurts from the stress,
Now she's just a mess.

She won't slip back to what she used to be,
'I won't let that happen,' she says, 'not to me.'
She's been left behind,
Her soul - she can't find.

She wants to be happy and let them all know,
But her brain won't let her emotions show.
She loves you, you see,
But she can't be who you want her to be.

She screams so loud, yet no one hears,
Can't anyone take away her fears?
Can she leave him behind,
So she's no longer confined?

She pretends it's all fixed and there is no pain,
But really, behind the smile, all there is is strain.
The lies are too strong,
What has she done that is so wrong?

She's scared how much she has altered,
It's him who did this, she shouldn't have faltered.
She wants to go back to before,
Because she knows she's worth so much more.

Emily Bevan (13)
Kendrick School, Reading

Indian Summer

Nanny cooking,
Grandma cooking,
Auntie cooking,
Mother cooking,
My cooking burnt.

Stealing mangoes from next door,
Telling off from Mr Balangore,
Saying sorry, fingers crossed,
He knows that we can't be bossed,
He doesn't really mind us.

Summer flies,
And mosquitoes,
Bees and wasps,
That sting your toes.

Playing with my cousins,
Naman, Bipul, Aditi,
Babies crying, want their food,
Sambar, chutney and idli.

When we're on the roof,
We all play Indian games,
Kabaddi and antaxari,
When we beat him, my dad's ashamed!

Electricity goes down,
Very, very often,
Children cry when lights go out,
But soon they start to soften.

Bathing in the Ganges,
Looking at cloudless skies,
As I board the aeroplane,
I say my last goodbyes.

Vatsala Mishra (11)
Kendrick School, Reading

My Best Friends

Liv and Mag
Mag and Liv
Where should I start?
I met them in the school corridor
And straight away they stole my heart

We've been through thick and thin
The thickest you can get
We'll be together till the end
I knew that when we met.

For the next few years we were joined at the hip
Bitching and having fun
We always mucked about in lessons
And called each other 'hun'.

Like a handsome ship we sailed the ocean
Nothing stood in our way
If anyone put my mates down
I'd have more than bad words to say.

We all went to uni
Liv got all the boys
Maggy got three PHDs
And my confidence changed to poise.

Now we sit here in our old people's home
Chatting and sipping tea
We won't forget the times we had
My best friends and me.

Jzuee Pradhan (14)
Kendrick School, Reading

Summer By The Sea

An
Intense
Burst of light
A coolness engulfing you
Sand in your pants
Swallowing you whole
Like quicksand
Waves
      C
       R
        A
         S
          H
           I
            N
             G

                  Against giant rocks
                  Drenching
                  The bystanders
                  With a white, foamy spray
                  Shouts of playful kids
                  Smell of the ocean breeze
                  And ice cream in my mouth.

Caitlin Green (11)
Kendrick School, Reading

Christmas Poverty

Leaves are falling off the trees,
Floating, flying in the breeze.
Brown leaves, red leaves, yellow and gold,
The weather's changing, it's getting cold.
It's the time of year when trees are bare,
Children come out to gaze and stare,
For on the ground, nothing does show,
As a sheet is laid of glistening snow.
'Hurray!' they cry, for it's Christmas time,
A time for family, fun and chime.
We play, we laugh, but forget one thing,
Not everywhere does this happiness ring.
For while you eat your Christmas dinner,
The children in Africa are getting thinner,
They're starving and cold, but with no one to help,
All they can do is cry and yelp.
So next time you have your afternoon tea,
Pray for the children across the sea.

Santthia Rajagobalan (12)
Kendrick School, Reading

Summer

Stroking the sun-line a pale azure,
Drenching the honey-glow,
Winking, a cloudless sky so pure,
The budding emerald, her golden cure,
Whilst nervous summer breezes blow.

Silky, caramel sands,
Stir on golden, foreign shores,
Whilst eerie gulls swoop through the lands,
Frost stallions of the seas,
Peer into aquatic floors,
In a mangled olive-green.

How obscene,
How blind of us . . .

Josephine Thum (11)
Kendrick School, Reading

Tide Rushing

(In the style of E E Cummings)

Tide Rushing -
waves are   green   brown
charging across mudflats before us
and we

run
footprints embedded in mud tide Rushing
water crashing at our heels
andwerunfasterandfasterandnever STOP
Until we throw ourselves
gasping

onto soft sand
staring at this   sea   Rushing tide -
so calm and slow   after
being so
tide Rushing rushing   Tide

Laura Hankins (12)
Kendrick School, Reading

Summer Horizon

Summer's here, bright and lively,
A kiss of sea breeze across my face,
The distant cry of seagulls fishing,
Far out in the blue lagoon.

The soft white horses eroding the rocks,
Creeping up the sand,
Washing away the summer's day
As the sun slips down beneath the land.

It's gift, a horizon of blood and crimson,
I smile my thanks into the sunset.

Oh, how I wish as I sit,
That this peaceful summer's day could
Last *forever!*

Lucy Barraclough (12)
Kendrick School, Reading

Summertime

The wind in my hair
And the sun on my face,
A wonderful glare
And a view that is ace.

A fabulous day
With a friend full of life,
'What beauty,' I say
A week with no strife.

'It's gorgeous,' we laugh
With a smile and a grin,
The heart of a photograph
So simple within.

We get off the plane
And we're back in the wet,
We'll see you again
I will never forget.

Samantha Wild (12)
Kendrick School, Reading

Tony Blair

Tony Blair
Likes to stare
He's kind of weird
And has no beard
Which makes him ugly
As he laughs so smugly
He hasn't started heaving
But instead he's happy to be leaving
To be Prime Minister is what he still longs
But now his home is where he belongs.

Ilona Onyango (11)
Newstead Wood School for Girls, Orpington

The Lady From The Library

She'd been in the library,
Behind her desk,
For almost seven years.
Her caring hand on the books,
Which have now grown dusty
And their covers worn away.
When she died,
They put up a notice,
For new library staff,
Got a bunch of lazy men.
There was a notice for her funeral,
So I went along.
Pouring with rain it was,
It was me, the vicar and the coffin.
She had no friends or family,
Only me.
A month later, everyone had forgotten
About the library lady.

Jessica Parker Humphreys (12)
Newstead Wood School for Girls, Orpington

The Owl

Burning eyes like a glowing spark,
Flickering side to side like a flame.
Eyebrows raised in an enquiring arc,
Encased in its feathery mane.

Silent in flight, but screeching in call,
Wings beat the still night air.
The murderous beak and grasping claws,
Warn all small rodents *beware*.

Burning eyes like hot desert suns,
Fallen onto the sand below.
When the morning appears, the night must be gone
And it brings the owl in tow.

Sibylla Kalid (13)
Newstead Wood School for Girls, Orpington

Unknown

No one cries at the unknown soldier's grave
No one weeps for that soldier, lone and brave
No one remembers what he may have known
Through darkness comes light that leads him home

A tree falls in a forest, it breaks on the ground
But if nobody hears it, does that tree make a sound?
A leaf of the willow tree drifts in the air
If they do not know it, how can they care?

In the shadow of a funeral, around the grave they stand
But a woman at the back, did she even know this man?
For a man she never knew, a tear falls to the floor
A man she never recognised, this girl is crying for

A rose that grows in snow is not a rose at all
For a girl so full of misery, it's hope that makes her fall
A bullet for her heart is a bullet for her life
The pathway to her happiness lies just beyond this knife

A silent melody in remembrance may help her find her way
The seed that lies growing in her heart helps her live another day
Black lilies in the vase feed her wish for too-soon death
'It is all this man's fault,' she cries, 'though we had never met'

Committed to her memory lies a flower from her past
And when she heard that he had gone thinks, *I have no hope left*
to last

And ever since he went, she has spent her days alone
Living in a house in the darkness, a house where nobody's home.

Finn Butler (13)
Newstead Wood School for Girls, Orpington

The Point Of Life

'What is the point of living life?'
I once heard my friend say,
'All we do is breathe in, breathe out,
Every single day.'

I said to him, 'I know not that,
But this I know for certain:
People don't breathe *all* day,
What about old Newton?'

'But why do we have all these things,
So many live without?
Do we need our mini-gyms,
Or sport teams' try-outs?'

'Today, we do, we are a world
That wants quick-fix solutions.
Although we did not years ago,
Are we not evolution?

Have we not solved problems
That we never could before?
Found cures for diseases, or
Travelled without solid floors?

This, my friend, is my belief
Of why we're in existence.'
'I s'pose,' he said, 'when put like that,
Life's nothing but pure brilliance!'

Naomi Gettins (13)
Newstead Wood School for Girls, Orpington

Thunder And Ashes

Ivory silk sifts through black ashes
It's all just smoke, destruction and death
The skies above open: thunder and crashes
Tears mix with rain and breath

Her midnight-blue eyes are cast to the sky:
Deep seas of nothing but sorrow.
She thinks about her final goodbye
How she'll never embrace tomorrow;

She'd never thought of the words to say,
When she found what time couldn't heal
She'd never thought of no sunny days,
Despite her heart of tungsten and steel.

Sometimes she'd walk across the lake,
Trailing ashes behind on her hem.
She wishes that joy were hers to take
She wishes that it were not condemned.

Inside her heart is eternally blackened,
But she keeps her dress snow-white:
It's a reminder of joy that slackened,
It keeps her asleep throughout the night.

The dark world around stubs her candle;
Velvet ghosts haunt her mind with guilt
The secrets and lies are too much to handle
If only roses did not wilt.

Writing words that'll never be read
She waits for the Grim Reaper.
Writing until every tear's been shed,
Her misery channels deeper.

Then the scythe came swift:
And she gave away her greatest gift.

Zoe Liu (13)
Newstead Wood School for Girls, Orpington

Friendship

Our friendship is like an ocean,
Deep and wide,
Filled with memories,
True and mild.

When I needed a shoulder to cry on,
When I needed someone to talk to,
You were by my side.

When I had no one to play with,
When I stood there single handed,
You came running over to my side.

When I couldn't run as fast as others,
When I kept on falling down,
You were there for me, encouraging me to keep trying.

When I needed someone to hug,
When I needed someone to share my victory,
You appeared like an angel sent from Heaven.

You were a priceless gift to me,
Worth more than gold.
There isn't anything that I wouldn't do,
To have a friend like you.

Shobika Mohamed (13)
Newstead Wood School for Girls, Orpington

A Poem

On a bench I sat and cried
I wondered, *what is the point of life?*
Someone said I'd no potential, but I so did try
When I was young, at the age of five
I was praised, but now my heart has fried
No one loves me and no one cares.

Life bit down so harsh on my gentle soul
My hopes and dreams shattered before my eyes
And life was cold like a lump of coal
All I want now is to hide away and lay down and die
I will curl up in a ball and live like a mole
No one loves me and no one cares.

As I lie on the damp grass, I ask
'What am I meant for, just to be tormented?'
I need to be alone, I don't want a task
I am sorry for my actions, I really mean it
Then emerges someone new, they hug me and say 'I love you'
Someone loves me, someone cares.

Bethany Appleyard (12)
Newstead Wood School for Girls, Orpington

Through The Fire, Through The Dark

I thought I could see when
I was burning up. I thought the pain
Healed my breaking heart.
Through the fire, through the dark.

I thought the hurting
Could make me whole. The crying would soothe
My aching soul. So I hurt and I cried;
Through the fire, through the dark.

I thought you were lying
You said it's not true. What I thought
Was misshapen and confused. And the blood, the tears.
Through the fire, through the dark.

I thought it wasn't real when
You held me tight. And gave me the strength
To win the fight. You helped me
Through the fire, through the dark.

Alanah Mortlock (13)
Newstead Wood School for Girls, Orpington

The Gang

Fat, they call me, loser, geek,
I know they hate me, but still
Popularity I seek.
If I got slim and did what they did,
If I became bad, if my personality I hid,
Maybe they'd like me,
Maybe they'd care,
Maybe I wouldn't
Be the odd one out there.
Got to stop eating,
I have to get thin,
Now for me being me
Is the worst possible sin.
I stop myself eating and make myself sick,
I don't answer in class, I pretend that I'm thick.
Just to get in with them,
Just to make friends,
I can't sleep for worry,
I toss and turn no end.
They still ignore me though,
In school and out,
They will never like me,
Of that there is no doubt.
I just cannot take that,
To be hated forever,
So now I've made my choice.
To live with that,

I could never.

Anna Westley (12)
Newstead Wood School for Girls, Orpington

The Real Me

My nose is big,
My bum is fat,
I eat like a pig,
I look like a rat.

My legs are hairy,
My eyes are small,
My thighs are *scary,*
I'm way too tall.

My arms are flabby,
My shoes are the wrong brand,
My clothes are all shabby,
My coat is second-hand.

I've got acne on my face,
But I can't afford the cream,
I have to wear a brace,
I have no self-esteem.

Lucy says I stink,
Brian says I'm crazy,
Barry puts my phone in the sink,
Florence says I'm lazy.

But if people got to know me,
I think that they would find,
I'm really quite ordinary,
Fun and clever and kind.

Harriet Sands (13)
Newstead Wood School for Girls, Orpington

A Haunting

She's sitting on her rocking chair,
Rocking in the dead of night,
Just moving back and forth.
And a cat to keep her company,
She just stares into space,
Her face, dead,
Blanking out the whole world around her.
Back and forth, back and forth,
Something may be haunting her.
What though?

At eleven every night,
She gets up off her rocking chair,
Waking up the cat.
Walks slowly up to the clock,
The chime sounds eleven times,
She looks up at it,
Seeing the pendulum swing,
Back and forth, back and forth,
Something may be haunting her.
What though?

Celine Lee (13)
Newstead Wood School for Girls, Orpington

Fire!

Under the thick blanket of darkness,
A small, bright spark jumps quickly to life.
It lingers playfully a moment,
Then bursts violently into flames.

These demonic tongues of fire,
Tear quickly through the bedroom floor.
I stand petrified and watch them,
As they surround me; I am trapped.

Dark black smoke is poisoning the air,
It is choking me, strangling me.
My weakened lungs feel frail and burnt,
Soon my helpless body will cease to breathe.

Here my burning corpse will lie forever,
And the tale will be told throughout the town,
Of the poor, young soul who screamed in pain,
But who no one ever came to rescue.

Geneviève Zane (13)
Newstead Wood School for Girls, Orpington

What Have I Done Wrong?

What's happening, Mother?
Why are there so many flashing lights?
What are they taking me away for, Mother?
What have I done wrong?

Who's that man with the funny hair, Mother?
Why's he so high up?
What's he doing with that hammer, Mother?
What have I done wrong?

I'm old enough now,
Old enough to be locked up.
Old enough to understand what happened.
Mother refuses to come and visit,
She thinks I did it.

But I didn't kill my father.
It was suicide.

Olivia Smith (12)
Newstead Wood School for Girls, Orpington

I Was Alone . . .

I walked along the road
Alone, on my own

No hands to hold
No eyes to see
No ears to hear
I was alone

No one to love
No one to hug
No one to talk to
I was alone

I had a life
But no point in having one.

Mina Thiraviyarajah (13)
Newstead Wood School for Girls, Orpington

Feelings

I shouldn't feel like this
I know it's really wrong
But I just can't help myself
This feeling is so strong.

No one else has noticed
That no matter what I do
I can't focus anymore
Because my thoughts are filled with you.

I've always looked up to you
Admired who you became
But a part of me still hates you
For being the cause of my pain.

Maybe if you had followed me
That day I ran away
I would have had the guts to tell you
That things weren't OK.

That they would never be OK
Not while you're still here
That things would only change
If I took a hold of my fear.

And told you how I felt
How I've felt all my life
But that might have made things worse
Added fire to the strife.

You have no idea how hard it was
Not knowing if you were alive
And I'm writing this to just make sure
That you managed to survive.

Alexandra Wheeler (14)
St John's Catholic Comprehensive School, Gravesend

Poverty

Poverty is a serious matter
It could be the reason lives shatter
Wait a minute, let me tell you why
Please try not to cry

P is for the unbearable pain
O is for the ominous hours of work with nothing to gain
V is for the value each morsel of food holds
E is for the embarrassment keeping them from being up front
    and bold
R is for the reassurance that never comes
T is for the tap that poisons so many dads and mums
Y is for you to help these people by just giving a little support

I is for the impatience that never ends
N is for the neglect that offends

T is for the terror of dying
H is for the hopeless dreaming and lying
I is for the ignition in so many hearts
R is for the rage ready to be released like a dart
D is for the dreaming that never comes true

W is for the wondering, *why me God?*
O is for the occupation that doesn't even pay enough for a stick
    or a rod
R is for the realisation that no one else really cares
L is for the loss of another child and a new stream of tears
D is for the diseases that kill

C is for the countless numbers of deaths happening all the time
O is for this ongoing, never-stopping rhyme
U is for the unnatural amount of pain
N is for the needed but never-coming rain
T is for the terrible journeys for a drink
R is for the roofless houses pushing families to the brink
I is for the infections that hurt so very dearly
E is for the empathy that people say they feel when they actually
only care rarely
S is for the shirts and skirts and scarves and socks and shoes
they don't really have.

It needs to stop now!
Give to charity
Help them to help themselves.

Jass-preet Sohal (13)
Slough Grammar School, Slough

The History Of Water

The past reaches out to me like an arm drowning in water,
Splashing droplets of water onto a cobweb over the bookcase.

When I see a photo, the people scream out, crying for help,
Reaching out to me like a child drowning in water.

Occasionally, something catches my eye, like a book out of place,
Floating out to sea with my thoughts.

Sometimes the dying fire is put out,
As it descends into the water.

After a while I feel alone, submerged in the water,
Letting out knowledge like a man who surfaces; exhales.

Often the past swims back to the surface; my mind.

Zahra Gain (13)
Slough Grammar School, Slough

Why Do They Do This To Me?

I was sitting there,
The tears running down my face,
Why do they do this to me?

My friends,
My foes,
They all mean the same to me,
Why do they do this to me?

My life,
My dreams,
It is all the same to me,
Why do they do this to me?

The anger,
The pain,
It all feels the same to me,
Why do they do this to me?

Sophie Long (13)
Slough Grammar School, Slough

World

A brush on a canvas
It can do so much
An image that can change the world
May be created with the movement of a brush.

It's a different world
The world of art
It's a world I can create
Rub out all the problems
Paint over the lingering hate.

The world of art is a quiet world
Entered when pencil is put to paper
Silently, I make my world
I eliminate the stress
Then the bell goes and I return to Earth.

Alice Schmitz (13)
Slough Grammar School, Slough

Pain

Poverty is full of pain
It should be stopped
But why is there poverty? I think to myself.

We laugh, we go abroad
And we are provided with food and shelter
But why is there poverty? I think to myself.

We go to school to be educated
And make friends and have laughs
But why is there poverty? I think to myself.

We go abroad to have fun, see beautiful places
And spend time with our families
We have a home to live in
Like a life full of Heaven or paradise
But why is there poverty? I think to myself.

This could finish by tomorrow
If only we took action, or took a step . . .

Gurneet Kaur Gill (13)
Slough Grammar School, Slough

School's A Prison

Why do we have exams?
Why do we have detentions?
What is the point of having them?

We want to have fun in our homes
This school is a hell of a prison
Alarms are around to stop us escaping

Why can't we play cricket all day?
This school has some bad times to work
We are innocent
Who makes us work all day?

The jail has the worst jobs
How can I live in this terrible place?

Vicknaraj Sahadevan (13)
Slough Grammar School, Slough

Maths

Algebra, sums, equations and pi,
These are the things that love, I
When I solve and expand the brackets,
I tell the teacher that I have hacked it.

X squared, roots and Y,
All you have to do is times it by pi,
Trigonometry, Pythagoras,
Are all very glamorous.

Even soh, cah, toa,
That all wear a boa,
The minus, the plus, dividing and the time,
Never ever work on the prime.

Sequences, prime numbers, don't forget nth term,
All makes my brain swivel like a worm,
English, science are wastes of space,
By far, maths wins the race.

Abu Miah (13)
Slough Grammar School, Slough

Secrets

Can I tell you a secret?
Shh . . . don't tell anyone.
The first time my stepfather
Laid a hand on me,
I was secretly glad.

I thought this would show my mum
He was really bad,
But she just looked at me
With hollow eyes
And told me to
Forgive and forget.

Ekta Namas (13)
Slough Grammar School, Slough

All Alone In The Darkness

All alone in the darkness, what will happen now?
Why did they bring me to this place, when, why and how?
Now they've brought me somewhere else, where all the others are
I'm really missing home right now, as it is very far.

I look around for reassurance, but that I cannot find,
All the others look depressed, I wish they could be kind!
What is going on? I think, as some are taken away
Good or bad, I couldn't tell and where they're going I couldn't say.

I start to go deep into thought and think about old days
When in my field I'd run and jump and buck and rear and play
I came back to earth to find something was going on
I heard a bang and that was it, there and then my life was gone.

Isobel Byrne (13)
Slough Grammar School, Slough

Have A Look At What It's Done To Your Mum!

Teenage pregnancies
Don't let it happen to you!

Everyone says it's really fun,
But people who say this are really, really dumb,
Just have a look at what it's done to your mum!

Each day you get bigger and fatter,
You might as well be covered in fish batter!

But still, everyone says it's really fun,
And people who say this are really, really dumb,
Just have a look at what it's done to your mum!

Symrath Virdee (13)
Slough Grammar School, Slough

Life

Life is a journey
To get through it
You need to enjoy it

Once you get to the end of the road
You will die and leave the world
You will go to Heaven
After you've been judged.

Life is a path as well as a journey
Choose a different path
And there will be a different story
Once you are down and out
You are like a car
You need to fill up
And get on the go
For more experiences tomorrow.

Once that journey comes to an end
You will fall
But God will catch you
And send you to Heaven.

This is life -
Live it
Enjoy it.

Life.

Arjan Singh Bains (12)
Slough Grammar School, Slough

Imagine

Imagine if life
Had no war or poverty
Things would be better

Imagine if life
Meant no discrimination
Everyone equal

Imagine if in life
Everything was perfect
And had no sorrow

But what would life be
If there were no problems to overcome?
How strange it would be

Life is not perfect
But we are blessed all the time
Life is precious

You may not be rich
But remember this message
Your life is a gift

Life is always great
So no need to *imagine*
Go out, live your life.

Lara Mackey (13)
Slough Grammar School, Slough

Suffering

The anger is from suffering,
It comes from all the pain.
The moment you witness for the first time,
The torment and the strain.
A strange feeling whirls around inside,
What would it be like if we had their pain?
We'd freeze,
We would be homeless, resting in the lane.
It makes you wonder,
How do they survive?
Then you think again,
Not many stay alive.
We do not like to suffer,
It makes us feel upset.
You are being bullied,
Given each and every threat.
It really is terrible,
What people do for fun.
Then you find the solution,
So in the end, you've won!

James Wickens (13)
Slough Grammar School, Slough

What Is Life?

We are lucky that there's a light,
Shining through the end of every tunnel.
For some this will never happen,
We achieve, we succeed.
Others in the world are left starving,
Crying and dying.
The life they live is dull, sad,
For us it's a start of something new.
Life is something we live,
We want, we dream,
But we hate what we have.

Amreen Dhanoya (13)
Slough Grammar School, Slough

We Learn Nothing From The Past

We learn nothing from the past
The past is just a distant thing
Worth nothing, just an echo of a dream.

We learn nothing from our past
What has happened cannot happen again
Or can it?
Can we reach out and pull the happenings of our past
Through to our present?

We learn nothing from any past
History repeats itself, or so they say
If only we could listen
If only we could learn
But we can learn nothing from our past.

Hannah Wiltshire (14)
Slough Grammar School, Slough

Give And Take

The ambiguity that's been crossing my mind,
Where is the charity I've been waiting to find?
Giving what you have and some of what you need,
As long as we're equal in colour and creed.
I want to give, but they won't take,
Their heart is beating, ready to break.
I give them money as a token,
Some have it,
Some left heartbroken.
Cos we live to die, but we die to live,
Don't be afraid to take what you give.

Arjun Jung (13)
Slough Grammar School, Slough

Life

Life is like a road, you don't where it's going to take you,
You can't let the other cars on the road take you where they
are going,
You are your own little car on the journey, you take you where
you want to be.

There may be many bumps and construction sites on the way,
But no matter how much damage there is,
Your little car will pull through if you want it to!

The cars around you will change as you grow up too,
The little toy cars you once knew could turn into four by fours,
Or they might still be your toy cars from playschool.

This journey might be tough, you might face some
extreme conditions,
But to get to your destination, you should be able to face them,
Don't let a bit of rain or people talking about you get you down!

Farhia Afzal (13)
Slough Grammar School, Slough

Africa

In Africa people are wild and free
But this is serious, no comedy
People are starving
They are really hungry
It's kinda lousy
That we sit and watch TV
No help for this poor country
Where people are forced to live in a shanty
Their hospitals are old and rusty
There's no safety
And we just sit and watch TV.

William Wright (12)
Slough Grammar School, Slough

All About Cricket

Cricket, cricket, cricket,
Try and hit the wicket,
Let's get a ticket
To see some cricket, cricket, cricket.

The bat is made out of willow,
But the batsman hits the ball like a pillow,
The batsman gets out,
And retires hurt from gout.

The fielders stand there for a catch,
Hoping to win the match,
If he catches the ball he is a hero,
If he doesn't he is zero.

The bowler bowls the ball,
Aiming for the tall Andrew Hall.
But he hits the bowler for a six,
And the umpire chills with a chocolate Twix.

This is the beautiful game,
With all the fame,
Cricket, cricket, cricket.

Manraj Jhalli & Jaskaran Sandhu (13)
Slough Grammar School, Slough

The Day You Let Your Feelings Shout

They say you have to have a way with words,
To write a poem or sing to birds,
But you will find this is not true,
For I will say this through and through;
The day you spoke,
Is the day I heard,
For on that day a poet spoke out,
That is the day you let your feelings shout.

Pavindeep Randhawa (13)
Slough Grammar School, Slough

Life

Life is a holiday
Life is a test
Life is your destiny
Life is a rest
Life is a package to make your own choices
So hurry up and make a decision
Life is short so don't take your time
Or you will be left far behind
Life is to show you are able
Your life is like a table
Life is to show you how to survive
And how it feels to be alive
Life is to explore
And to be happy to follow the law.

Manveer Singh Chander (12)
Slough Grammar School, Slough

Life

Live,
Your death is guaranteed,
Do not refuse it,
Do not abuse it.

Your time will end,
So you must comprehend,
Make the most of living,
Your life can change in a split second.

So get up from your chair,
Don't stand around and stare,
Have a dream like Martin,
Amaze thousands like Lennon,
Change history like McAulife.

It doesn't matter if you fail,
God will catch you.

Live.

Sahib Singh Dhillon (13)
Slough Grammar School, Slough

Life Is Liveable

Before your birth
Your destination is the Earth
But do you wonder what it's worth?
Now think about your life
Make sure that you create no strife
Minds all work in funny ways
If your mind wanders, your body stays
To show peace, we use a dove
And friendship is a kind of love
But what do you think of your life?

Friends are the family that you choose
So why not let your friendship ooze?
Your life was given for a reason
So don't just use it for one season
Your life is special, so use it well
Your life is not something to sell
Life is life.

Whilst you live
You should give
Whilst you sleep
You should dream deep
Whilst you walk
Why not talk?
Never think of dying
Never think of crying
You may think death is near
It's a thought you need to clear
You have a life to live.

So now you've reached your destination
There's no time for hesitation
Enjoy your life!

Nicole Edwards (12)
Slough Grammar School, Slough

Have You Ever?

Have you ever felt like you're looking for something
But you don't know what it is?
Because I have.
Have you ever been silenced by your own words?
Because I have.
Have you ever been looked at funny?
Because I have.
Have you ever felt a rush of joy?
Because I have.
Have you ever jumped off a cliff?
Because I have.
Have you ever lived on the street?
I have.
Have you ever gone to sleep hungry?
I have.

Even though I've done all this
And you may not have,
We are all human and we are all the same.

Arif Javed (12)
Slough Grammar School, Slough

My Dog

He came to us so small and fluffy,
He was so nervous he wouldn't come out,
He wouldn't even play when we gave him a ball.

He very slowly grew,
Into a mischievous little thing,
He kept us on our toes.

When we started taking him for walks,
He would go and play with other dogs,
All we could see was his tail waving in the wind.

Then off home we would head,
He would then scoff his face
And then he'd head off to bed.

Jack Glen (13)
Slough Grammar School, Slough

Life: Road To Nowhere

Life is a path, a journey,
There are many paths to take,
You must take one,
Every path leads to another.

You will go through many emotions,
Love, hate, anger.
You will feel all of these some time or another,
To anybody, anything.

All paths lead to death,
One that we all must take,
Then!
Silver shards of glass.

Life is an endless journey,
There is no final destination.

Douglas Naylor (13)
Slough Grammar School, Slough

Kidnapped Kid

They're alone and they're cold,
They're staying in places that are mouldy and old.
No toys to play with, no food to eat,
They have dirty, bare, slashed feet.

Once she was a jolly girl, playing at home,
Now she's a dismal girl all alone.
Once there was laughter and fun,
Now a greyer life has begun.

At home there's a family waiting, wishing, hoping,
Searching for their child, only just coping.
They're unstoppable in their search,
Determined to find their little girl.

Ela Berksoy (13)
Slough Grammar School, Slough

Life Is . . .

Life is like a great long road
Knowing what you have been told
Yet living the life you want to lead
With equal colour and equal creed
Life is about fulfilling your dreams
And all that it means
For all the laughter and all the tears
For all the hopes and all the fears
Taking each day as it comes
Helping many people, not just some
Life is like the desert, open and free
But to be happy you need to know what it means to me
Life is thrust upon you as a gift given to you
But by whom? Me or you?
Every day things and people change
Sometimes good and sometimes strange
The only way to unlock your life is with the keys
Because the only thing that stays the same are our memories.

Rachel Smith (13)
Slough Grammar School, Slough

Death From The Heart

I wake up and wonder if it's still a dream,
Droplets tip down, smudging the cream,
All of those good times pass through my mind,
Cherishing your thoughtfulness and how you were kind,
I wonder if you are listening to me,
Sitting in sadness under a tree,
I wish and wish that you would come back,
And fill the empty space on my rack.

Rachel Abebrese (13)
Slough Grammar School, Slough

Life As It Is

Life is like a person,
A person you cannot describe.

Many things make up life,
Each life is different in its own way.
Some lives you cannot describe.

Life is full of love and care,
At the same time,
Full of hatred and hostility.
Life you cannot describe.

So why try?
You are happy,
You are sad,
Feelings you cannot describe.

So leave it,
Leave life as it is.

Rupa Suresh (12)
Slough Grammar School, Slough

Snow

Snow, the bright surface, so very clean to the eyes
But the truth is hidden just like a spy
Gleaming, glowing, oh no, it's snowing!
A few hours later the children come out
They throw huge snowballs and they start to shout!
Little do they know that later in the day
All that snow will be gone away
By about 3 o'clock, that pile of snow
Will turn all grubby
Then the kids will say 'Snow, just go away!'
The ice is getting to my toes
Snow is the last thing I want to see
I hate snow!

Nitharsan Theivendran (13)
Slough Grammar School, Slough

My Earth

I overlooked a giant sphere,
Free of human inequity.

I threw myself forward,
A soft sensation.

The world was still for a few seconds,
And so was I.

A jerk borrowed my attention.
It was nothing but my dog, Lufus.

A satisfied atmosphere,
I was content and happy.

My life could end and I'd be gratified,
But never! Not on a dirty, spoiled Earth like ours.

Bombs, bullets and buckshot.
Dictators, destroyers and deceit.

Injustice, internecine and inequality.
Abuse, abduction and anxiety.

Nevertheless, I commend great leaders of the world,
People who are selfless and humane.

Ghandi,
Martin Luther King and
Abraham Lincoln.

I lift my head to the stars,
Against my comfy pillow.

I lie on my bed, calm and still,
Realising I'm down to Earth.

Joshua Heslop (13)
Slough Grammar School, Slough

Late Again

Is that the time?
I must get up
Brush my teeth
Have a bath
Get changed
Comb my hair
Eat breakfast
Go to work late as usual
Get in the car late as usual
Drive to work late as usual
Enter work late as usual
Say hello to my mates
But then I see
My boss who is always angry at me
Fires me . . .

No work
No income
No home
In debt
On the run
From the law
Don't have the money
To pay the debt
Must steal
But it's against the law
But I need the money
Go abroad
Become an illegal immigrant
That'll teach me
Never to be late again.

Deep Lall (13)
Slough Grammar School, Slough

What Would Happen If TV Was Gone?

What would happen if the TV was gone?
Every single person would moan.
Kids would come home every day,
Only to find the TV's gone
And they would find it very wrong.
There would be no news,
We wouldn't find out what happened to Mr Clews
And soon boredom would take over us,
All we could do is count people in the bus.

It would still be boring,
Chavs would be kept at home,
They'll get on the streets and roam.
More graffiti,
More pity,
And still we would be bored to death,
The chavs would get hooked on crystal meth.
Then - everyone remembers the cinema,
The rush would increase with everyone wearing Kevlar.
So the destructive chavs wouldn't hurt them
And the cinema company would flourish forever.

But still there would not be the satisfaction without TV.

Siddh Maru (13)
Slough Grammar School, Slough

What Lies . . . ?

What lies beneath the crusty grass which lives upon a hill?
A rock-hard shell
Or lonely cell?
They stay there all so still.

What lies within a volcano just waiting to erupt?
Some red-hot slime
All in my mind
Just sitting there corrupt?

What lies behind a brown closed door in an empty house?
A pale, white ghost
The missing host
As quiet as a mouse?

What lies beyond the stars that are in the dark blue sky?
An alien race
A comet at pace
That all do fly so high?

What lies below the seabed that's home to lots of things?
Some thick black oil
A snake that is coiled?
In the sea the creatures are kings.

Rosie Byne (12)
Slough Grammar School, Slough

What Has It Become?

A girl merrily playing pretend games on her own
Suddenly, *snatch!* and she disappears into thin air
Where has she gone? Nobody knows
Her parents in tears waiting anxiously for news
Will they ever know?
What has it become?

A few friends just chatting casually
Then all of a sudden . . .
Bang! Bang! Bang!
A man standing there with a gun in each hand
They're all gone, nothing but memories left
What has it become?

They hide behind the walls
Praying for it to end
Gunshots echo in their mind when they sleep
The only thing keeping them going
Is the thought of their families and duty to their country
What has it become?

Life can be cruel
What the future holds, nobody knows
Live each day to the full
Enjoy what life brings
Don't ask what it has become
But make it what you want.

Amnique Dharwar (12)
Slough Grammar School, Slough

Emotions Around Me

Hearts racing, blood boiling
Red-hot and blazing
Like a violent volcano erupting or a burning fire
Anger is all around me.

The sun shining high up in the sky
Bright, vibrant and yellow
Happy thoughts and smiling faces
High-pitched laughter in the air
Happiness is all around me.

Crystal tears pouring down unhappy faces
Hearts filled with pain and sorrow
Silence in the air
Sadness is all around me.

Envious eyes, electric-green with jealousy
Evil, like a vicious snake
Jealousy is all around me.

Cold, shaking hands
Pale with fear and terror
Almost as white and fragile as paper
Fear is all around me.

Every human has emotions
Whichever emotion it may be
Emotions are all around me.

Justine Chileshe (11)
Slough Grammar School, Slough

War

No doubt this war is for oil and money,
We kill innocent people because we think it's funny.

I think we have overstepped the human barrier,
For the sake of lust, nationalism and our career.

Injustice, inequality and racism,
Has made people think about what they wear.

9/11 or 7/7,
Who's going to Hell or Heaven?

This is not a question at this time,
But who's behind the scene of war and crime?

Bombs destroying the world from east to west,
Has made the world a humungous mess.

No matter what we do, it's how we behave,
War and peace will never be the same.

Walk on love and peace passage,
Because this is my last message.

Hasnane Chohan (11)
Slough Grammar School, Slough

Dreams

Dreams, everyone has dreams
Mine are with light beams
I know it makes no sense
But mine are filled with suspense
My dreams have sadness
My dreams have darkness
But isn't that what the world of today
Is filled with?

Navraj Singh Rehncy (13)
Slough Grammar School, Slough

Cars

Cars are like Quality Street, everybody has a favourite
All shapes, all sizes and any colour you can imagine
From SUVs to sports cars
Any style you prefer
Teenagers with Golfs
To old people with their Escorts.

Cars, how they have changed
From three wheels to four
Six valve to twenty-four
Dump valves, tinted windows
Alpine stereos, DVD screens
Air bags, brakes, turbos
Spinners, engines and automatic cars.

We take cars for granted though
By speeding in them
And crushing them with monster trucks
Without cars what would we do?
We couldn't walk from Southall to Slough
Or meet friends and family
We would have to use a train or boat
But if we did, they would be packed.

So enjoy, but respect this invention
Cars, which one's your favourite?

Harvinder Singh Dhillon (11)
Slough Grammar School, Slough

Broken Shell

All my life
I have stayed in my shell
Abused, neglected, bullied
But now that shell has broken
I can feel all the anger rising up inside me
Nothing can stop me now . . .

Manpreet Dhuga (13)
Slough Grammar School, Slough

The Spark Of Life

Where does it start?
The battery-powered lifespan
Does it start with dawn or dusk?
Does it start with nature or Man?
Life is like a battery
It's not everlasting
Like a firework starting off
And in the air it goes blasting.

How it takes its time to fly
Going off with a light
How it eventually comes to an end
And presents its ending with a flash so bright.

Memories fade
Memories return
The candle slowly continues to burn.

A story begins
A story grows
For hundreds and hundreds of lifetimes it flows.

Where does it end?
The battery-powered lifespan
Does it end with a full stop
Or a question mark?
Does it end with the blow of the wind
Or the angels?
Hark!

Avneet Gill (12)
Slough Grammar School, Slough

The Road Trip

I don't claim to know it all,
I've had some wins, I've had some falls
The road is long, the time is short
I don't want to spend too much time in thought
I'll walk it all; I'll take it slow
I'll reach my goal; whatever more
I wasn't born for small-talk towns
I know what I want and it's not in this town

But I don't want to just survive
I'll start a car, start to drive
My friends are there, they'll help me strive
The journey's long, my strength is great
I'll do my best and then do some more
I don't intend to play it safe
I'll reach the end with pride in place
So I'll just keep going the way I've gone so far

The road is long; the time gets shorter
I don't want to stop at my best;
I'll keep going until the end!

Tanya Hossain (12)
Slough Grammar School, Slough

A Dazzling Sunset

Golden light,
Shooting through a crimson sky.
Colours blending,
Magic for your eyes.
A burning star,
Disappears, a lie.
This is the start of night.

Neelam Sidhu (12)
Slough Grammar School, Slough

Deal With The Difference!

Walking down the street,
An ordinary day,
What I hear and see,
Brings me dismay.

Black and white,
They're both unlike
To get together
Without a fight.

Asian or African
Tall or small,
Does it really matter
What you look like at all?

Fat or thin,
They both have skin,
Both different colours,
So who really wins?

Ethnic origins,
Disparate and diverse,
People got to deal with the fact
Not everyone's the same in this universe.

Diversity is what should bring our world together,
People should stand together,
So do your part and let people know, whatever colour or size,
Racism should be kicked out forever!

Aqsa Hussain (13)
Slough Grammar School, Slough

Today, Tomorrow, The Future

Throwing litter, driving big old cars
Polluting the world
And causing global warming
Without thinking about
The future.

Killing innocent people
Without caring
Tomorrow we can end
With a dirty, unclean
And lifeless world.

Instead, we could start caring
About the environment
Stop pollution, stop wars
And start to live in a better
And more peaceful world.

Umar Hakim (12)
Slough Grammar School, Slough

Open Your Eyes

They are hungry for food and water
Hungry for love
Hungry for a roof over their head
Hungry for clean clothes

Nowhere to go
Nowhere to say
No parents
No friends
No one

Open your eyes
Help them
Help them soon.

Wiqas Ali (13)
Slough Grammar School, Slough

Politricks

We went to war in April,
They said they'd kick out Saddam.
They acted like they cared,
But they couldn't give a damn.
That's politricks.

And what did we get out of this?
Nothing, that's what.
We're a terrorist target, we weren't before
And that says a lot.
That's politricks.

As for the environment,
They should do as they say.
The ice caps are melting,
It's pouring in May.
That's politricks.

We've had panic scares,
For SARS and bird flu,
DEFRA can't fix it
And neither can you!

For something to change,
They must tell the truth,
And before they arrest someone,
They gotta have proof.
That's politics.

Catherine Morris (12)
Slough Grammar School, Slough

Friends

Friends are like family
Caring for you all the time
Brothers and sisters are also
Caring for you all the time

If you're high or low
Whatever you're feeling
Your friends are there to be with you

Just like the Musketeers
If you're broken
You will get fixed

Friends were unimportant
Friends have been unwanted
But somehow they have always been wanted.

Fat or thin
Strong or weak
Big or small
Coloured or not
Don't differ from yourself.

Treat them like family
Whatever their race
Colour or size.

Aaminah Hussain (12)
Slough Grammar School, Slough

Why Chelsea?

How do they do it?
How does the crowd scream and shout?
That's the question
Well, the answer is because . . .
They support Chelsea, the greatest football club around
So why do I support Chelsea?
Is it Cech?
Is it Lampard?
Is it Terry?
Is it Drogba?
Or is it the special one?
Yes, but also the cheer of the crowd
The atmosphere at the Bridge
The players' consistent shots
And mostly . . .
Chelsea's pride to play the game
I feel the passes
I feel the powerful, game-winning finishes
And I certainly feel the bone-crunching tackles to win the ball
The other player falls
And Chelsea go on to win the League again!

Alex Friston (12)
Slough Grammar School, Slough

Different Me's

You see me, standing here,
Staring at you,
Why can't I tell you I love you?
You're like a disease,
A painful memory in my head I can't get rid of.

I'm sick of you, you've hurt me,
Made me grieve over you,
You're a heavy weight on my shoulders,
But all you wanted was not me.

The memories I have of you are all good, why?
You're so loveable, you're a weakness,
You rejected me, but I still hold you dear.

Agitated by how much attention you bring to yourself,
Why can't you be like the rest?
Don't stand out.

You make me glum, just thinking of you,
Why her? Why not me?
I know I'm not all that, but I thought I was something.

I make many propositions, but you reject them.
Do you know how stressful it is,
Knowing the guy you love and care about,
Thinks poorly of you and wants nothing to do with you?

Just give me one chance, you never know,
Can't you change?
Stop me loving you,
Because . . . you! You! You are the reason!
You make me upset.

You dismay me all the time!
Act like I'm not here.
You wish I wasn't, but I can't change that!
Unless . . .

Letitia Powell (13)
Slough Grammar School, Slough

Words

Words can spark the imagination,
An army of them can influence the mind,
Together they can build poems, letters and speeches,
Everyone is addicted to using them.
There are bad words, good words, long words and small words:
The addiction of a word is like the addiction of a breath,
No one can stop you from speaking,
Words can be seen, words can be heard, words can be felt,
Words can also be a part of our instinct, our lives,
They have been spoken in a thousand languages
And a billion times over.
There is always an option to use when it comes to words,
Expression goes in, they are part of your soul,
They show your character, they can change you:
New words are being made and the old are being erased,
How did words begin?
How did we understand each other?
How did we begin to learn other languages?
Twenty-six letters in the English language,
Combined they make eight billion words.
Some words are used to explain others,
Some words are used to hurt
And some are used to comfort,
Some words can be seen through gesture,
Some words can be used to stop a poem.

Amar Dusangh (12)
Slough Grammar School, Slough

India, Beautiful India

India, beautiful India
The smell of mixed spices in the air, *mmm,* gorgeous
The funny sight of the cheeky monkeys swinging from branch
                                                to branch
In the untouched and native jungle areas
The tigers resting under the coconut trees
India, beautiful India.

During the school hours
The children working hard to please parents, teachers
                                and themselves
Parents rushing around, zooming through the market
Getting fresh foods for their evening inside
School ends, girls giggling with each other
Boys playing marbles under a shady tree
India, beautiful India.

At home, home sweet home
Getting ready for the sparkling and magical ceremonies
Mums and dads partying with each other
Everyone enjoying themselves
Warm welcomes from everyone
India, beautiful India.

Damini Panesar (13)
Slough Grammar School, Slough

Him!

I get home and there is no one there,
I see flashbacks from yesterday
When his screams pierced through my ears.

The door slams downstairs,
I'm left with only my fears.

My heart begins to sink,
I know he's had not only one drink.

I wish Mum was here,
I miss how she'd care
And call me her cute little bear.

I have a drink of water,
Why did I have to be *his* daughter?

My hands are shaking,
I feel as if I'm baking.

The glass drops,
I rush to get the mops.

It's too late, he heard the smash,
Now it's me who'll get the bash.

He sees what I've done,
Apparently I did it for fun.

I back away slowly,
There is no other way.

I see how he builds up his rage,
There's no escape from this horrible cage.

Next thing I know I am on the floor,
Is it over now?
I can't be too sure.

Blood trickles down my head,
I can't move to get to my bed.

I huddle in a corner,
I still feel as if I'm in a sauna.

I remember how he calls me a rubbish heap,
Like every day,
Once again I cry myself to sleep.

Kanwal Balouch (12)
Slough Grammar School, Slough

Claw

My name is Bird,
I fly in the sky,
The weather is pleasant,
I fly above the mountain, sky-high.

Soaring above the sky,
I see my prey,
I am so happy to see one,
But it runs away.

I am a hawk,
My life is to fly in the sky,
I fly so fast,
Cutting through the air like a knife.

The breeze is cold,
It makes me feel like I am back in my nest,
Having a good rest,
But there's no time for that,
All that I do is look for food.

My eyes are like a camera lens,
All I use them for is to search for my prey,
When I see one, I have my life!

Karanvir Singh Uppal (12)
Slough Grammar School, Slough

Lost

Imagine having lost someone very special
It must be excruciating
You must be hurting so much
That you have no more tears to cry.
Just imagine.

That person who was once in your life
Has gone away to Heaven
But even though they're gone
You will never forget them.
Just imagine.

Think about them
Cry for them
Love them
You know you would do anything to turn back the time.
Just imagine.

One last time to think about who got you into this mess
That person has brought you and your family so much grief
But you know you must forgive
But you can never forget.
Just imagine.

Rebecca Lathey (13)
Slough Grammar School, Slough

The Great World Of Football

From an abysmal performance last week,
Kaka struck hard.
And drilled the ball into the back of the net,
Sending Milan soaring to the Champions League final,
Booting out Man Utd in the process.

We chased all season,
With high hopes,
We believed we could.
Tremendous setbacks swept over us,
In the end though, we remained second best.

Brazil fought and fought,
The defence sparked up trouble,
Old pensioners losing their pace and stamina,
But they are still as ever at the top,
Thrilling the crowd with their fantastic goals.

So that's football for you,
Joy and despair.
I know it doesn't sound fair,
Some teams have great stealth,
But this sport isn't good for your health.

Mohamed Choudhary (13)
Slough Grammar School, Slough

Why Don't You Just Think?

Wholesome winds, brilliant breeze
The ones that tickle around your knees
Gales that travel from overseas
Powerful and troublesome, never to cease
Why don't you just think?

Holding hands, loving life
A break away from bills and strife
One moment that seems so nice
Passion as sharp as a butcher's knife
Why don't you just think?

Repetitive ranting, danger delved
Hate always leaves emotions shelved
The victim is in the user
Not in the abuser
Why don't you just think?

Dangerous death, torrid toil
Unnecessary things begin to uncoil
Wanton killings, blood to boil
Could it really be about oil?
Why don't you just think?

Stopping and starting, flawless flailing
Always people constantly failing
Always people constantly prevailing
Life is never plain sailing
So, why don't you just think?

Lost life, fallen friend
People that are a godsend
The victim is impossible to mend
Death comes at the end
Why don't you just think?

Terrence J Fendley (13)
Slough Grammar School, Slough

It

Around the world it goes
Up and down
Here and there
Bearing more than a thousand humans' weights
Doing its job dutifully
And proudly
With brave deeds attached to it
Although it can take lives
No one is frightened to try it out
It makes its passengers amazed
Though it can leave them dazed
Making a terrible racket as it leaves
Eyeing all the little kids who wave at it
Ignoring them as it climbs up higher
Through the clouds
And up, up and away . . .
Looking down on moving stick people
Engulfing more clouds as it ascends higher
Feeling heavier as the hungry passengers inside fill their stomachs
And slowly doze off . . .
One by one, till every person aboard is snoring
Then it comes to a point where it is high enough to do nothing
Apart from travelling straight on
Soon, as many sleepy people start to stir
Everyone is aware that it will start to descend slowly
After that it will be time . . .
Time to depart and say goodbye
Hoping to meet it again . . .

Sharvari Khapre (13)
Slough Grammar School, Slough

Outside Of This World

There are places outside this world that are unimaginable,
'Heaven and Hell',
Heaven has love and beauty,
Hell has scorching fires
And the smell of burning flesh.

In Heaven you can have anything,
In Hell you are condemned to one,
Pain!
In this world if you do good deeds,
They will lead you to Heaven.
In Heaven you have great weather
And clothes made of the finest silk.

Hell is deadly,
Containing all sorts of creatures,
Snakes, dragons and even monsters,
All biting you,
Tearing you apart.

And so my friends, take heed of my words,
For you have one life.
Heaven or Hell awaits you!

Do good for then you should go to Heaven.

Hasan Iqbal (12)
Slough Grammar School, Slough

The City

In the city of London it's very busy,
Especially in the morning,
People arrive to the bustling, noisy city,
To work and talk to and meet people,
There is commotion and excitement and happiness.

There are many cars and buses,
The fumes of which pollute and stuff the city,
And people wonder why there is global warming,
The trains come in and leave,
Creating colour with the trees, buses, cars and trains.

People are busy eating,
Busy getting fit, busy working,
All around you there are people in suits,
Everywhere, high achievers,
Everyone is on the phone, on the computer,
Dashing everywhere -
But why are they in such a rush?

Yet, as people are so busy,
No one notices the beauty of the city,
The architecture, the river, the monuments,
People stay oblivious to the beauty.
The city itself stays silent,
With the people making all of the noise.

Sara Siddiqui (13)
Slough Grammar School, Slough

Food

Food and me
Live happily
So that we can show
How to make people healthy

However, there is still a lack
Because food doesn't just appear in sacks
In Asia, Africa and South America
So together, let's get rid of famine forever

Then there is obesity
People are getting fat easily
Is McDonald's to blame?
Either way, it's all the same

As we see food's good and bad
All the problems make me sad
But I still love food
(Especially Galaxy bars!).

Ahmed Magid (13)
Slough Grammar School, Slough

Summer's End

The long summer months bring out sea and surf
Long, sandy beaches and inflatable boats
But cooler mornings and dewy turf
The reluctant trip to school with bags and lightweight coats.

White-clad gentlemen with bat and ball
Spend clubhouse evenings drinking long, cold beer
But days grow shorter and brown leaves fall
The umpire and friends depart for another year.

But excitement builds and shadows grow longer
Familiar heroes march before the crowd
The game begins and the roar grows stronger
Young children and parents cheer aloud.

The floodlights shine, the games end in draw
Happy fans celebrate the first win of the season
The pitch disappears with our throats all sore
Happy supporters celebrate beyond all reason.

Heated conversations in pubs
'The ref cheated us, I cannot believe those cheats'
We hurry past the arguing and mindless thugs
And prepare to do it all again next week.

It's now 10 o'clock, time to go
Train, bus, car, travelling away from the dome
I wake up again and the year has gone so slow
And summer's back again, I'm here, I'm home.

Connie Parris (13)
Slough Grammar School, Slough

I Wish My Place Was In Space

Every night I look up at the stars,
Wondering what is out there,

Whether there is any life out there,
Or just black emptiness,

Whether there is anything beyond our universe,
Or nothing,

Whether it will ever be normal to go to space,
Or never,

Whether there is an orange sun,
Or red,

Every night I look up at the stars,
And it makes me think of our world,

The stars have no corruption and pain,
Our world has a lot,

The stars have no cheating and envy,
Our world has a lot,

The stars have no hatred and jealousy,
Our world has a lot,

The stars have no slavery and labour,
Our world has a lot,

Every night I look up at the stars,
And hope that their worlds haven't been ruined like ours.

Talvinder Bal (13)
Slough Grammar School, Slough

A Poet's Heart

Away with words, just let my feelings flow
From the bottom of my heart to yours
Look at yourself and look at the people that need help
In one tick their world has gone while yours is still alive
You may curse God for being who you are
But when you look deep inside, with just a little bit of thought
You will find you have the perfect family.

Love, laughter, care and safety is all you need
Love laughter, care and safety is what they may never have
Don't just look at their tears, but the cry of their hearts
Feel their emotion and make them a part -
A part of time, a part of life
That only *you* can give to them.

Their pain will be forever running through their minds
Just look at them and take a little moment
To understand the hurt of their eyes
For they don't deserve what they have
Imagine how your world would be . . .
Take away their darkness and show them light
Wipe away their tears
Only you can make this better, with the depth of *your* heart.

Bhawna Sharma (12)
Slough Grammar School, Slough

The Evil In This World

Is there really a God in the evil of this world?
At night I ponder, twist, turn and curl.

With rape, death and even war,
I wonder, can I take it anymore?

Underground I see the Devil and he speaks to me,
'There is only war, you'll end up down here, you see!'

I pray to God to deliver us all,
But have I earned or am I destined to fall?

And the nuclear missiles launching all over the world,
I stand my ground and allow my true intentions to unfurl.

I'll fight for God, shouting, 'Bole so nihal',
My soldiers behind me screaming, 'Sat Siri Akal!'

I'll have my kirpan in my hand and God on my mind,
There'll be no stopping me, that's what you'll find.

I'll fight for my freedom,
That's my main reason.

I'll fight for my religion,
That's my sub mission.

Don't mourn for me if I die on my mission,
Being a martyr has become a part of my religion.

And when my deed is done and my body lies on the field at night,
Hear my prayer, save my soul, Lord God, please take me to
Your light.

Sanjiven Singh Aujla (13)
Slough Grammar School, Slough

Naïveté

It's funny how when it rains it pours,
Got money for wars, but not to feed the poor.
It's funny how people discriminate,
Others take the bait, and meet their fate.

People dying ev'ry day,
Gangs don't give a damn 'bout what they say,
Their situation, their circumstances, their events in life,
'No more chances!'
They scream at them, hold a gun to their head,
'One more word and I'll shoot you dead.'

Don't want your kids to join them,
Cos you fear for their lives,
Next thing you know, they're smoking and carrying knives,
Ready to attack anyone who steps outta line,
They no longer know wrong from right,
To them it's all fine.

Do anything to gain respect from their mates,
A shooting, a stabbing, a coupla rapes,
A corner shop robbery of a dozen sweets,
Leads to burglaries for 'homies' treats.

It's funny how when it rains it pours,
Got money for wars, but not to feed the poor.
It's funny how people discriminate,
Others take the bait and meet their fate.

Bilal Baig (13)
Slough Grammar School, Slough

I Had A Vision

I had a vision
That the world was pure
I had a vision
That war was no more
I had a vision
That no man was sore
I had a vision

I had a vision
That the world was right
I had a vision
That there were no more fights
I had a vision
That there was always a light
I had a vision

Then I realised
You have to face reality
You have to play your part
And face fatality

I still have faith
In that one true vision
Even if there are faults
In that decision.

Vidhu Sharma (12)
Slough Grammar School, Slough

Reason

I did not see
The point of it
To extend the sea
It does not fit

To reason

I did not know
Why to unleash
Such horrible woe
Out of the sheath

Of reason

Why when water arrived
Death was launched
So Death could survive
It could not be fought

By reason

I could not understand
Why when water surged
And consumed the land
People did not surrender

To reason.

Friedemann Schack (12)
Slough Grammar School, Slough

Snowman

I'm as cold as the mill glass,
As still as a dead heartbeat,
Friendless, like an Ethiopian child,
These who created me, abandoned me,
They treated me like I was a heartless piece of meat,
I thought I was family,
Until I saw them eating their Christmas meal without me,
Without my presence,
I am crying, even though the tears are not falling from my eyes,
And when they do, they freeze, along with the rest of my body,
I am camouflaged with the heavy snow,
My mind is as cold as a slice of ice,
I watch the kids as they run to school,
I wish I could move even one inch of this ball of snow,
But I'm helpless,
Thoughtless,
Friendless,
I stand here alone,
Neglected,
Unwanted,
Unappreciated.

Moiz-Ali Zubair-Dar (13)
Slough Grammar School, Slough

Pressure

My heart was bulging into hyper mode,
Pressure was mounting load by load,
Everyone was depending on me,
With all this pressure I was in piles of agony.

The cold, disturbing wind was thrusting against me,
The soggy pitch was effectively a sea,
The pitch was more or less a ditch,
I was more or less handicapped to take this penalty kick.

My team had all the confidence in the world that I would score,
Not me,
So much is depending on this lifeline kick,
For if I score we won't be relegated - if I don't I will be hated.

From hero to zero?
Or from zero to hero?
The ref blew his whistle for the penalty kick,
My eyes lit.

Yes!
Tucked in away nicely,
I'm a hero . . .
I'm so relieved I wasn't Mr Zero.

Aneil Persad (13)
Slough Grammar School, Slough

9/11 - The Twin Towers

We all know that date . . .
Which was full of terrible sorrow and hate,
Where amazing skyscrapers fell from the sky,
Where thousands of innocent people had to die.
Horrible monsters hijacked the planes,
That crashed into the towers with burning flames,
The day we will never forget.

Mothers and fathers,
Aunties and uncles,
What about the children?
All died without saying goodbye.
The towers fell from over a thousand feet,
Where the top of the twins and the ground had to meet.
There was a thick black blanket in the atmosphere,
People around the world shed a million tears,
The day we will never forget.

The people inside fell to their grave,
The towers fell down, unable to save,
People lying under all the rubble,
Crying in their own little bubble.

On that day the world came together,
To commemorate the death of citizens forever,
We shall never forget the hurt and pain,
That happened on that traumatic September day.

Annabel Oakley-Watson (12)
Slough Grammar School, Slough

Life

It's as if it could all end at any given time,
No warnings or signals, just drop and die.

Nans and grans, closest to you,
They're the first to go, even though they love you too.

But think for a moment, how have you helped?
Have you stopped a crime or turned around a frown?

With all this trouble on the Earth,
From global warming to stealing your purse.

But I have a saying, that once a day,
Do something good and keep evil away.

But it doesn't work, not all the time,
Because when you need it most, it retreats to its vile prime.

Some people let it go, do as they want,
From killing people to doing what they can't.

This isn't what life is about,
Just stop it all, no scream, no shout.

Remember with just the flick of a wrist,
Nothing about it, stops with a twist.

Life.

Christopher Newman (13)
Slough Grammar School, Slough

Just Because

Just because . . .
Just because I wear make-up, doesn't mean I'm conceited
Just because I straighten my hair, doesn't mean I'm self-centred
Just because I get my nails done, doesn't mean I'm a tart
Just because I like to take care of my appearance, doesn't mean
I'm fake

Just because . . .
Just because I act loud, doesn't mean I'm an attention seeker
Just because I say what I think, doesn't mean I'm over confident
Just because I like to shake my bum, doesn't mean I'm out of control
Just because I'm me, doesn't mean I'm fake

Just because . . .
Just because I hide my feelings, doesn't mean I'm not hurting
Just because I smile, doesn't mean I'm not suicidal
Just because I don't frown, doesn't mean I'm not angry
Just because I act strong, doesn't mean I'm fake

Just because . . .
Just because I hug the boys, doesn't mean I'm slutty
Just because I talk with the boys, doesn't mean I'm a flirt
Just because I laugh with the boys, doesn't mean I'm 'easy'
Just because I'm friendly, doesn't mean I'm fake

Just because . . .
Just because you decide to label me, doesn't mean I'm like that
Just because you think I'm a certain way, doesn't mean I'm like that
Just because you assume I'm plastic, doesn't mean I'm like that
So go ahead, label me all you like, you'll do it anyway.

Lucy Sackett (13)
Slough Grammar School, Slough

What Do I Want?

What do I want?
This is the question I've been asking myself all these years
What do I want?
What do I want?
Do I want happiness for my family
Or that scholarship to go to the States?
Sometimes I want a name, fame, money
And other times a little bit of happiness for myself in my life, for once.

Civil wars, terrorist attacks
Do I want them to stop, or just carry on?
It's madness
What do I want?
I am so confused
I feel like shouting out loud
What do I want?
My mum says I should study hard to get into Oxford
My dad remarks 'just relax'
'Chilling' in my language.

Life looks so fun if only I could enjoy it freely
What do I want?
One day I'll have to make up my mind
And that day shall be today
I have decided that I want . . . um . . . um
Everything
Oh no! I still can't decide what I want
My wantings will never stop
I will have more passion for other expensive, small and new things

So I shall carry on my quest to find
What I do want!

Ritika Kochhar (11)
Slough Grammar School, Slough

Peer Pressure

It all started in the class of glorious mathematics
Madame Burns was rounding up our homework
I did mine and extension to quality that of a professor
She slowly walked up to me as her high heels clicked
'Young Sir,' she started, 'what have you got for me today?'
I proudly popped my work into her pile and her smile widened
I did so much work that when I put it into her pile, her veins
                                                    popped up

After school these boys confronted me
We had a little chat
They gave me a proposition that they said was unbeatable

Then, later that night, after school my mother came up to me
'Clean your room up, darling, it's getting a bit messy'
She looked at me as if she was waiting for an answer
'No,' I said, 'I don't want to. You do it, why should I?'
I couldn't believe I was saying this
'How dare you, young man. That's it, no pocket money for a month'
'I don't care!' I roared
I had never shouted at her like that
Instantly, she knew that there was something wrong and asked me
I said there wasn't, but she knew there was and made me spit it out
'It's these boys,' I mumbled. 'They said I should be like them'
'What type of boys are they?' she asked
'They're really cool, popular and um . . . um bad'
Her jaw dropped instantly, 'Why would you do this?'
I told her that they'd let me hang with them
And in reply I had to do their homework
My mum wasn't pleased and gave me advice on what to do

At school the next day, I walked up to Danny and Mike
I had a second thought of what to do and just let it out
Right in their faces I shouted, 'No deal'
They backed off and walked away
They said that they weren't going to let me hang with them
But I didn't care, I was back and it felt good.

Bhavraj Rehal (12)
Slough Grammar School, Slough

Love For You, Mum!

(I dedicate this poem to my mum)

Thank you for standing by me through thick and thin
For never giving up on me and consoling me with a grin
As you reared me with care and watched me grow
It is sad to know that one day I will have to let you go

When I'm weak, you stand by me and become my strength
To fulfil my dreams and needs you'll go to any length
When I'm lost and lonely you'll get me back on track
When I'm down your kind talks will bring my confidence back

When I awaited my exam results you gave me hope
When I was struggling through life you taught me how to cope
When I had given up completely you led me through miles and miles
When I didn't believe you brought back my smiles

Your love is like a package sent from God with great care
This love is like no other with which to compare
And I just want to let you know that my love for you will never die
And I can tell you my love is true, I cannot tell a lie

I adore the times we 'mess around' and joke together
And I hope and pray that these memories will last forever
In you I know I can always confide
My mood swings and tantrums you do abide

I just want to tell you that you came in the form of a hero in my life
And through life your love will continue to give me strength to survive.

Aarti Joshi (13)
Slough Grammar School, Slough

21st May 2007

I can feel the blood pumping through my fingers
I can hear my heart beat faster
It gives me the will to write and learn
And feel
Red-hot is running inside me
I feel inhuman, indestructible
Charged

You come in my way?
Be warned
I am not what you see
I am different
I see things from a different perspective
I look at things with a different eye
I view things that come from another world
I am alive

Don't stop me - I've only just started
The rain trickles down my face
Inside me, there's something I cannot name
For my thoughts are on exodus, leaving my brain

I am different
I am alive
I see what others don't
I am not confused, bewildered or ill
I am here
I am me
I am unique.

Harveen Hayer (13)
Slough Grammar School, Slough

Why Me? Why Me?

Why does this always happen to me?
Why was I born this way?
What did I do to cause this pain?
I suffer every day

Why me? Why me?

Nowhere to go, no one to talk to
Dirty water to drink and no food to eat
I'm ill, but I have no money
Wishing to get off my feet

Why me? Why me?

I work hard all day to earn a living
But at night when it gets cold
I stay in my bed all alone
But 'Go to sleep' is all I'm told

Why me? Why me?

Through my life I saw a lot of flaws
I learnt to smile through this sorrow
But through all this rain and pain
I hope to see a better tomorrow

Why me? Why me?

Karishma Jhandey (12)
Slough Grammar School, Slough

Today Is The Day Of Judgement

Today is the Day of Judgement
There is only one obstacle in the way
In order to achieve my goal
I must play

Today is the Day of Judgement
The world number one to beat
And as time goes on
More people take their seats

I was really nervous
My palms were full of sweat
There is a gloomy task ahead of me
I knew this was a test

Today, the Day of Judgement
I am ready.

Ishan Rashid (13)
Slough Grammar School, Slough

War Is . . .

War is bloodied soldiers, dead or battered
Dreams of a peaceful world, shattered
A gunshot echoes, the last private falls
Blood-spattered houses, with blood-spattered walls.

Doom and destruction, contained within a shell
Shrapnel and debris rains, all is not well
Helpless civilians caught up in warfare
What once was an urban preserve is gone, but where?

Civil war and lethal battles, all caused by oil
For one gallon of the liquid results in turmoil
Wanton abuse and gloom-encrusted trouble
The aroma wafting in the air, the repetitive stench of rubble . . .

War is these such things.

Ajmal Singh (12)
Slough Grammar School, Slough

The Rainy Day Blues

Looking out of the window,
On a rainy day,
'Go do some homework,'
I hear Mum say.

How do I tell her I want to get out of here?
To go travelling to places both far and near,
So far to drop off the highest heights,
Longing for less of those sleepless nights.

Whilst I lie in my bed, far from asleep,
I feel my shadow ready to leap,
Thinking . . . wishing . . . waiting for tomorrow,
Hoping it will bring an end to this sorrow.

Just as I see the morning sunrise,
I get out of bed and waste sighs,
And as I guessed, another rainy day,
'Go do some homework,'
I hear Mum say.

Jasmin Rai (13)
Slough Grammar School, Slough

Litterbugs

Every time I look around,
I see some litter on the ground.
Oh, I just don't know where to begin,
All this litter on the floor,
Don't think I can take much more.
So I pick it up and put it in the bin,
In the end I pity the fools,
They'll get a 'litter pick' after school,
Then hopefully this madness will stop.
People think it's cool,
To drop litter around the school,
Boys and girls, I tell you it's not.

Kyle Watt (13)
Slough Grammar School, Slough

Expectations

Life is a simple matter,
But for some it is complicated.
At a point in life, you must miss a beat of your heart
And you think to yourself, *have I done my part in this world?*
At least I'm expected to.
We all have expectations.
Will I succeed?
All of that hope we have is concentrated,
The one thing we are so scared of.
We think, *am I the only one?*
Will I succeed?
It's like riding a bike, you cycle up a steep hill,
Feeling up to the challenge,
And with all your might, you achieve that feeling of success
When you reach the top.
We expect to with each trial we pass,
We get the successful feeling
But . . .
During a tough challenge we have expectations
And we feel nervous.
Don't let that get to you!
Never forget, too much confidence and you will not succeed,
Be too nervous and you will fail.
Never forget, we all have expectations,
Never forget, we all have expectations.

Joseph Muller (12)
Slough Grammar School, Slough

If Only . . .

Here lay a girl, lullabying herself to sleep,
Leaving the realms of sanity,
Burying her head in the arms of destiny.

She knew she was the one chosen,
To have this ill fate. Bear this sorrow.
Still her eyes, incandescent with rage,
Still her heart, swelling with mourn,
Still her mind, filled with merely one thought,
Revenge.

She cursed his decision,
She cursed his army,
She cursed the lieutenant who had taken her life away
Yet left her alive.

Left with the hushed night air to nurture her,
The relentless waves to father her.
Often she thought, there was no need
For these precious tears to flow,
For these aching nights to continuously taunt.

If only he had,
Abolished the thought of war,
Welcomed the thought of peace, into his mind.
If only . . .

Shriya Prabhakar (12)
Slough Grammar School, Slough

The Kick

I wasn't in a good position,
I felt like the world was on my shoulders.
Standing there waiting for the time to come,
When I would shout in happiness or sadness.
Waiting for that rush of happiness I was,
Knowing that it may stay in the abyss away from my grasp.
I met the goalkeeper's eyes,
Our enmity was open to see.
He glared and so did I,
We readied ourselves for the kick,
The great deciding kick.
It didn't matter to the goalkeeper,
If he didn't save it,
No one cared,
But if he saved it he'd be a hero.

That's the thing about the game,
The wonderful, wonderful game.
The whistle, it blew,
I took my run up
And struck the ball with all my might.
Terror spread throughout my body,
Like a deadly, infectious disease it took its toll.
Before the result, I knew what had happened,
My hopes of euphoria had vanished.
Into the veil of darkness it fell.
The ball thumped the crossbar.
I missed,
That was it -
I missed.
But we still won in the end!
My kick was the first.

Baljeet Singh Lakhan (12)
Slough Grammar School, Slough

Our Own Reality

I come home on Monday,
With my concerns, anxieties, troubles trailing behind me.
Tugging on test revision,
Drawing behind a detention,
Hauling my homework.
I stagger into my room
And collapse onto my bed,
Falling into darkness . . .

Just when I think there is no end to the abyss,
A burst of light penetrates the darkness.
My rational thought tells me, *don't let everything get to your head!*
I say, *how do I escape it?*
It's a black hole of despair!
It says, *remember our reality . . .*
Your reality . . .

The darkness shatters,
Illuminating the universe behind,
As bright as desire,
A world of opportunity.

This exists in everybody.
The hard part is finding it,
But it's the best possible existence
And it delivers, as I received,
The most unbelievably wonderful revelation.
Life is only bad if you think it so.

Akrist Sainju (11)
Slough Grammar School, Slough

My Exam Fear!

I stand outside the hall,
My fingers freezing too,
I try to think calm,
But I really don't have a clue.

I am shaking with fear,
Teeth clicking loud,
I try to chat to a friend,
But I am way too nervous.

I swear I've forgotten my revision,
I know I am going to fail,
I can't think straight,
And I think I've gone all pale.

I stayed up for hours last night,
Trying to get it right in my head,
I called Mum to help me,
But she said, 'Just go to bed.'

The teacher comes out in silence,
'7R,' she screams out,
I take my first steps in,
Knowing I can never go back again.

45, 46, 47, 48, 49 . . .
I finally find my seat,
The exam is put in front of me
And I have freezing cold feet.

I've finally finished the exam,
And I think my mum was right,
I've done all the questions in time
And there was no need for the fright.

Kiran Suri (12)
Slough Grammar School, Slough

When I'm Older

The thing is . . .
What do I want to be when I'm older?
A teacher!
A teacher!
A teacher?
Teachers are boring,
Teachers are crazy,
Teachers are fun,
Teachers are lazy.
What will everyone think?
She's dull,
She's mad,
She's stupid,
She's sad.
What subjects?
I like doing art and technology,
I'm OK at maths,
I'm good at biology,
I'm good at English, what should I do?
Who should I teach?
2-year-olds,
5-year-olds,
10-year-olds,
Or even 15-year-olds?
Am I capable?
I love children,
I love to play with them,
I love to talk to them,
I love to read to them,
Will I be a teacher or will I be taught?

Ayeesha Vithlani (12)
Slough Grammar School, Slough

Saving The World

The ice cap is melting,
The air is polluting,
The sun is shining,
The world is heating.

The people are burning,
So why don't we start learning?
Because everyone is suffering,
Due to the things we are doing.

Machines should stop working,
Because they are causing global warming.
Carbon dioxide flying,
Life is finishing.

Scientists studying,
What is happening,
Trying, stopping,
The world's ending!

Mariyah Zarine Akhtar (12)
Slough Grammar School, Slough

Time

Time is never-ending,
It is out of our control,
We spend forever chasing time,
It is our eternal goal.

Time is feared by many,
It shouldn't be wasted away,
It is very valuable,
As your time could be up any day.

Time flashes past when you're having fun,
But it crawls by slowly when you're cheerless,
It is a very powerful thing,
Use it well and you can face it fearless.

Time can be lost so easily,
Once gone it cannot ever be found,
You can never get back yesterday,
So make the most of today!

Amber Mahal (13)
Slough Grammar School, Slough

My Love For You

Through rain, hail, sleet and snow
There's nowhere I wouldn't go
There's nothing I would not do
To show my love for you

From the day we met, right from the start
You became the beat and pulse of my heart
You're my world, you're everything to me
You give me strength to be the best I can be

You're my rock, the essence of my soul
My destiny, the reason to reach my goal
That you've a heart of gold, with love so deep
I give you my heart, it's yours to keep

You're my life, my ray of sunshine
When I'm with you, I'm on cloud nine
And with these few words I want to say
Have a lovely, wonderful, miraculous day.

Bikram Narang (12)
Slough Grammar School, Slough

Nukes

Hydraulic rams opening a concrete jaw,
A shining spear facing the heavens,
Underground beavers cooped up at their stations,
You've been given your orders, it's time for war,
And unleash the Devil on unsuspecting nations.

A tailed comet arcing across the sky,
Finding its way with an arcane sense,
Its aim as true as a Sherwood shot,
There's no shield strong enough for you and I,
And it's no use running, it's just our lot.

A glowing fungus up high past the clouds,
A tsunami wave crushing all before it,
And on its spray Lord Death surfs,
He'll make his kingdom under black silk shrouds,
And bestow on the Earth his most deadly curse.

James Foster (13)
Slough Grammar School, Slough

Murder?

The darkness of the night,
The spiders that give you a fright,
The dust bunnies that bite,
It all comes out tonight.

The monsters that scare,
They might be anywhere,
The blood on the floor,
The axe in the door.

The finger on the table,
The dead sheep in the stable,
The white eye of the moon,
The lights out so soon.

The dim light in the room,
The broken flying broom
The creak of the door,
The 'eek' of the floor.

The lump in the bed,
Congratulations, you're dead!

Sunia Dhami (12)
Slough Grammar School, Slough

Gone!

The ice is gone,
The sun is shining,
Now there's none
And there's no lining.

The white fluffy creatures,
Are no more,
With tiny eyes and other features,
Lying on the ice-cold floor.

The friendly polar bears,
We thought we would forget,
Now are scarce,
We now regret.

It is our fault,
The polar bears are nearly extinct,
If we just halt,
Halt and think.

Natasha Sheena Patel (12)
Slough Grammar School, Slough

Is There Any Point?

Sports
Played on holiday, at home, at school
Why? Are we all fools?
They may not be the same
But they are still a dangerous game
Broken ankles, broken arms, broken legs
Body parts with metal pins, metal needles, metal pegs
These sports, is there any point?
Except a broken limb, or a dislocated joint
Yes, it's life
Putting up a fight
Life is for fun
Whether you talk politics, work or run
It's an experience
Which we can share
Love, cherish, care
Don't sit doing work all day
Enjoy your life
Be happy and play.

Tom Bond (13)
Slough Grammar School, Slough

A Poem

The idea of becoming a teenager,
Can sometimes get too much,
Worrying about exams,
Spots, or maybe a crush!

But then again it can be fun,
Being a teenager that is,
Popularity, style and friendship,
Or maybe the science whizz.

Of course there are bad things,
About being an adolescent too,
These things are so uncool,
Such as homework and secondary school.

But what crazy stuff do teenagers really do?
Maybe house parties and going wild,
But from all of this information about teens,
I'll stick with being a child!

Simran Tiwana (12)
Slough Grammar School, Slough

Friends

(Dedicated to all my friends)

Friends put a smile on your face
Friends tell you jokes and make you laugh
Making your day brighter and brighter
Friends will always be there for you
Especially when you're down
Even through the worst days, they'll be there
Watching you through and catching every tear
You love having them around.
But sometimes . . .
Some friends are not as true as others
The moment you turn your back
The knife comes out
And the friendship has died
But one thing is for sure
Without friends . . . life is not complete.

Maryel Decelis (13)
Slough Grammar School, Slough

Size Zero

They think it's the fashion
They think it's in
But what's really happening . . .
They're throwing their lives in the bin.

They're dying
Just skin, no fat
They can't see what they're doing
They're as blind as a bat.

They can't see the truth
They think they're pudgy
They need to eat
Some cake and fudgy.

They're dying, they're dying
They're close to death
They need to hire
A gourmet chef.

Katie Colbran (12)
Slough Grammar School, Slough

Stars

Twinkling in the moonlit sky,
Against a background of velvety darkness,
Sparkling like glitter
Being sprinkled onto a picture,
Peering down like eyes gleaming in the distance,
Shiny, silent, stars in the sky,
Waiting to appear in the night,
Graceful and gentle,
Searching, searching,
Just to find some stars
So you can make a wish that will come true.
So this is a song about stars,
There are so many words to describe stars,
Too many things to say at once,
Look for stars . . .

Mandy Bohan (11)
Swakeleys School, Uxbridge

Devil

Rapidly, wildly snapping at the long tails of grass,
Dramatically, leaping and springing to life,
Proudly wailing at the moon at night,
Dinner might be caught tonight,
Hidden in shadows and burning fire,
Waiting for the prey to approach.

Red, mighty, gleaming eyes,
Always staring at you . . .
Crushing and turning the meat into dust,
With those bloodstained teeth,
This furious, fearless creature,
With the red coat of armour.
Wolf! Devil! Wild as a wolf . . .

Sandeep Bansal (12)
Swakeleys School, Uxbridge

Dolphin

Shimmering and elegant,
It pirouettes above the glittering, blue sea,
Like a dancer performing on stage,
In a pool of blue light,
Playfully leaping,
In a captivating world of love and joy.

Flowing fearlessly from plant to creature,
Vaulting high into the air, plummeting down again,
Like a gymnast cartwheeling to the applause of the sea.

Soaring through a rainbow of water,
Glorious green seaweed,
Perfect pink pearls,
Soft yellow sand,
It glides through the warm, mysterious ocean.

Erin Patterson (12)
Swakeleys School, Uxbridge

My Cousin Emily

M inx, that's what she is
Y o-yo, my baby cousin

C uddles like a soft teddy bear
O bviously she is dead beautiful
U nique in her own little way
S he is just a little me
I love her in so many ways
N aughty little girl, takes after me

E mily, my little baby cousin
M y little shining star
I love her so much
L ittle angel she might be, but has a devilish side
Y oung and free, she runs wild.

Jasmin Bennett (12)
Swakeleys School, Uxbridge

We Will Meet Again

You're my best friend
You are always in my head
Like music lyrics playing over in my brain
I want to see you
But I can't
When will the time come?
I look in your eyes
I see someone
On the inside
A child still inside
Although you are older
I can see your inner spirit
Will you let it out?
Will you relive your childhood?
If you will, will I be there?
Smile at me
For when we become closer friends
We will meet again
Happier than now
Smiling into each other's eyes
Cheering on the inside
Letting our spirits out
Refilling those gaps
In the childhood we never had
We will meet again
And be in contact
For the rest of our lives.

Paige Brooks (11)
Swakeleys School, Uxbridge

Summer Days

Hot air
Sun beats
City streets
In the heat

Summer here
Once again
Come and play
With all the men

Mum shouts
Pool screams
Children playing
Very mean

School's out
Once again
Children playing
And making dens

Beds call
Children crawl
Up the stairs
And then fall
Asleep.

Zoë Brown (13)
Swakeleys School, Uxbridge

Sisters Forever

What would I do without my sisters?
What would I do?
What would I do?
Even though they can boss me around,
What would I do without my sisters?

My sisters are fun,
My sisters are cool,
One is in year eleven and about to leave school.
The other's in college, going to university.
Sisters are forever, like stars in the sky,
What would I do without my sisters?

What would I do?
What would I do?
Both of them are so different.
One's a piano, the other's a drum,
One likes action, the other likes comedy,
One likes R 'n' B, the other likes a mix.

Danielle McCammon (12)
Swakeleys School, Uxbridge

Life

Once upon a time, that's what they say,
Searching for that one special person every day.
Searching wide, across and above,
I believe living is more than love.
Education, family, friends and fun,
You can't just walk, you need to run.
Take the changes you are given,
Live your life.
It's not just about a husband or wife.
You are like an ocean, you come and go,
If you have any troubles, you know what to do and where to go.
You can't just walk, you need to run,
So love your life and everyone.

Hannah Dutton (11)
Swakeleys School, Uxbridge

Lean On Me

There's a man
Standing on the corner
He has no home
He has no food
Blue skies are gone
Can you hear him crying?

And there's a boy
Wishing he was free
No cure for his disease
As he looks up at his mother
She holds his hands
Praying that some day the sun will shine again
And the pain will end.

I am here, you don't have to worry
I can see your tears, I'll be there in a hurry
I'll be there to catch you when you fall
Here's my shoulder, you can lean on me.

Desree Gbejewoh (11)
Swakeleys School, Uxbridge

Cat

I love my cat, whatever she does
She loves me back
Even when I'm angry
I would never give her a smack.

She's as soft as a cheetah
Especially at night
Whenever she's sleeping
It's a very cute sight.

She's a little angel in the day
At night she's nowhere near
She's walking the streets
She has everything to fear.

Laura Hatherly (11)
Swakeleys School, Uxbridge

Chocolate Cake

Chocolate cake is such a delight,
I wish I could have it every night.
It's as soft as a rabbit,
As smooth as the sea,
I wish I could have it
Every time I have tea.

I could eat it all my life,
Yesterday, I ate about five.
I love it so much,
I have it for my lunch.
Chocolate cake is such a delight,
I wish I could have it every night.

I could eat about a dozen,
I even share it with my cousin.
It is so deliciously soft,
I even sometimes eat it in the loft,
but that's only when my mum says I've had a lot;
But chocolate cake is still such a delight
And I wish I could have it every night.

Fizra Rahim (13)
Swakeleys School, Uxbridge

My Cat, Amber

Breathing deeply,
Elegantly purring,
Her fur coat as soft as a grizzly bear,
Not wanting to be disturbed,
Needing her beauty sleep,
Her soft pink nose as dry as snakeskin,
Her paws touching my face,
Smooth, but rough.

Francesca Barker (12)
Swakeleys School, Uxbridge

I Wish I Were . . .

I wish I were a flower,
So I could blossom, grow and bloom.
I wish I were a single tear,
So I could release, realise and resume.

I wish I were a summer's breeze,
So I could dance with the gentle sun.
I wish I were the blue, cooling sea,
So I could watch the calming, rolling waves call.

I wish I were a smile,
Spread upon a young child's face,
So I could feel the joy and innocence
And love instead of hate.

I wish I were a poem,
So I could tell people how I feel.
I wish I were someone different,
So I could make your wishes real!

Faye Peters (13)
Swakeleys School, Uxbridge

The Dad Of Dreams

The time we spent together
Here on Earth
Enjoyment and surprise
Day after day, always together
Forever Dad, I miss you
Dad has gone round to God
Aiming at me
Miming I love you
Sensation of sadness builds up.

Sophie Matthews (11)
Swakeleys School, Uxbridge

The Four Seasons

Spring is the season of new beginnings,
lots of chocolate
and bingo winnings.

Summer is the season of the sun,
everyone comes out to play,
to have lots of fun.

Autumn is the season of many shades,
squirrels climbing up the trees,
everyone playing in the breeze.

Winter is the season of crystal snow,
glistening on the ground.
Every night it begins to glow.

They are the four seasons
coming every year,
going without reasons
but then the next is here.

Kimberley Newton (12)
Swakeleys School, Uxbridge

Childhood

Childhood is the best time of your life,
You don't have a care in the world,
You can do what you want,
Whenever you want.

When you're only three,
You can get away with being naughty,
You find new experiences like mud and bugs,
It's all love.

As you get older, parents get controlling,
You're struggling to break free,
Childhood is great.

Avneet Gill (13)
Swakeleys School, Uxbridge

Hidden Within

Within are my feelings locked tightly inside,
Inside of my baggy shirt,
Which shows no figure,
Behind all my pale skin,
Hidden inside.

People shout abuse on my route to school,
Psycho,
Weirdo,
Loser am I.

I sit in my form,
Misunderstood,
But I'm not alone,
For I have friends.

So I have no bad life,
Average from day-to-day,
I'm just tired of being hidden,
Hidden in the shadow of my peers.

Years,
Far too long,
Years I have sat like this,
We sit like this.

And I am not the only one,
Many like me,
We shall conjoin
And form a broken hearts parade.

Rebecca Adams (13)
Swakeleys School, Uxbridge

Lonely

Sitting in the darkness,
The quiet and lonely darkness,
Snow has fallen,
And covered the ground,
Shivering silently,
No food,
No drink,
No company,
Nobody cares,
Nobody remembers,
The noise of traffic,
People's feet,
Drumming the ground,
Everyone ignoring,
The dark, lifeless shape in the corner,
Tucked up in a cardboard box,
Fighting a losing battle,
Thirsty,
Hungry,
Tired,
People yelling,
Never silent,
Nobody wanted him,
For he could be nothing,
But an unwanted, little brown dog.

Esther Wiltshire (12)
Swakeleys School, Uxbridge

The Hunter

Ever so slowly she crept
Her paws sneaking through the jungle
Waiting till the right time and then she would have leapt
Pouncing on her prey and her meal.

Her gleaming fur, like the sun in the sky
Her teeth as sharp as knives
And then down she did lie
To watch her cubs jump and play.

They fight then they play
They leap from rock to rock
Then fall in the warm water of May
And then get wet, so they moan.

And so who is this magnificent beast?
Is it a lion?
Well, we know at least
That it isn't a dog.

No one will see this fearsome animal
For she sneaks around
With her fellow mammals
Camouflaged by the black stripes on her back.

Caroline Henderson (11)
Swakeleys School, Uxbridge

Susie Macane

They say she was one
The small, little child
Never had fun, never had fun

A small, little voice
Unhappy and scared
Nothing at all
No noise, no noise

Everything gone
No home, no life
Everything black, empty inside
Not even a song, not even a song

This little girl
Susie Macane
Has a small pearl she holds in her hand
Again and again

When you look at her
All you'll see
Is the fingermarks on her right cheek

She sits on the ground
In a corner down there
By the other side
With her swishy, blonde hair.

She looks around
So weak, so weak
Then before you know
She disappears . . .

Into the darkness
Into the mist
No one can see her
With her clenched tight fist

Susie Macane
No longer alive
With her swishy, blonde hair
At her side.

Shehara Vancuylenberg (13)
Swakeleys School, Uxbridge

Poem

Thinking today,
I want to change,
All that happened yesterday.

Sobbing tears, all came flowing,
Down my face last night,
I was really only wishing,
That I did stand up and fight.
I felt my views,
All securely in my heart,
I wish I could watch previews
And know when to change my art.
It hits me hard,
That I should have courage,
Not have my feelings barred,
Or locked away in the garage.

I have hidden too long,
All that should come out,
Never felt this passion,
No time left to pout.
I'm going out there now,
To change everything around!

All I ask now,
Is that you pray,
That everyone thinks *wow!*
And that this passion will never fray!

Elizabeth Surguy (14)
Swakeleys School, Uxbridge

The Apes Of Change

Three million years ago, in a land of dangerous things,
Cam an asteroid of destruction, chaos with it it brings.

Dinosaurs, monsters, do-dos, wiped out by an explosive boom,
In a land of burnt trees and craters, this land is full of doom.

The air covered by a dark, black cloud, so dense you can
                                        hardly see,
Then a dark, shadowy creature appeared from behind the tree.

The figure looked quite hairy, its chest perfect to bang,
And as it yawned a tired yawn, it showed a monstrous fang.

The ape moved across the plains, exploring the damage cause,
He came across a carcass, lifted it then paused.

The ape turned and carried on, past the polluted land,
And reached for the bamboo plants with an outstretched hand.

Slowly but surely the others joined in, no more eating meat,
Instead of a small mammal, they ate a veggie treat.

They developed really quickly, they began to lose their hair,
But those who still age meat, their body hair was still there.

Their arched backs began to straighten, their teeth began to
                                        shrink inside,
Things began to change, like their ears and eyes.

Growing an extra finger, even an extra toe,
They began to know things they didn't know.

The ape gave an almighty howl as the transformation came to
                                        a close,
He looked at his pale skin and felt an urge for clothes.

Men, women, children alike eventually have evolved,
But yet, the mystery of evolution has never been solved.

Lauren Browne (12)
Swakeleys School, Uxbridge

Breakdown

Did you want it to end this way?
Did you have it all planned?
Were you looking forward to the day,
I got up and ran?

Right out of this door,
Nothing to hand,
To end up emotional,
In this sullen land.

My imagination growing,
I started to learn,
The Lord was worth knowing,
That's where I turned.

Serena Hayes (14)
Swakeleys School, Uxbridge

Over The Top

Rifles loaded, bayonets fixed
As we stand here in this ditch
Waiting for the whistle to blow
Over the top and on we go
And as your life flashes before your eyes
You just have to wonder why
We ever had to face these guns
In a war that will never be done

Trudging through a field of mud
Now red with dead men's blood
Their bullets give no quarter
As we march to our slaughter.

Nick Fothergill (14)
The Oratory School, Reading

For The First Time

Ypres, 1917 -

Dear Diary,
Today was my
First day of combat
In the hellhole, 'wipers'.

I lay in my bush, hours
On end, waiting, just
Waiting.

My heart was pounding,
Faster and faster.
My hands were slipping on the stock,
My eyes blurred
And at that moment,
The heavens opened.

A helmet emerged over the enemy's trench.
It rose silently, stealthily, slowly.
I sprang to life.
I took aim and closed my finger
Around the trigger.

I squeezed and the shudder
Ran down my spine.
That inch of death flew through
The air.

There was a muffled thud
As it hit the German.

I am a killing machine.
Oh, what have I done?
He was only young.

Rupert Knight (14)
The Oratory School, Reading

Bloody Battle

As the metal flies
All of the widows cry
As all of their husbands die
Because of the bloody battle

The tanks roll on
The soldiers march on
The fortifications strong
During the bloody battle

So, why do we fight?
Our friends all take flight
All the soldiers dying left and right
People are disgusted by the bloody battle

Even now in these times of negotiating
The bombs even more devastating
With a flick of a switch, obliterating
The bloody battle shall never cease.

Oliver Wolf (14)
The Oratory School, Reading

England

E nglish is the language
N ational pride
G reen field
L and of Hope and Glory
A nd the flowing rivers
N ature and all its glory
D evon cream teas

E xtremism
N ightly drunken brawl
G oths, emos and pikeys
L itter flowing out of the bins and onto the streets
A ggressive youths drunken and abusive
N uggets and turkey twizzlers
D readed pollution in the big cities.

James Owen (14)
The Oratory School, Reading

Invasion

It was a regular school day,
With riots in the class,
When evil fiends invaded
With machine guns made of brass.
They assassinated all the teachers
And stuffed them down the loo,
They regretted this idea,
When they started to overflow.

They then moved on to years 7 and 8,
And lured them out with bait,
The screams died down
As one by one,
The children all turned brown.
One remained and ran
Into a wood,
Where he started a rebellion
With all the weapons he could.

He had a Tommy gun,
A knife and a trap,
Which when stood on,
Would make a leg bone snap.
He fought and fought and yelled,
Blood was everywhere,
He didn't stop until all the fiends were dead.

Jack Banbury (12)
The Oratory School, Reading

Poem

There was a great team called Man U
But they lost it all in 02
They scored some goals
And beat up Cole
The greatest team I ever knew

They were always top of the table
Everyone knew they were able
But then Vidic pulled Van de Sar
And Smith broke his car
The greatest team I knew

There was a great team called Man U
But they lost it all in 02
When Doyle got kicked
And Butt saw a click
The greatest team I knew

There was a great team called Man U
But they lost it all in 02
When Ronaldo cheated on Rooney's chick
And Neville became darkly sick
The greatest team I knew.

Carl Annan (13)
The Oratory School, Reading

Candle

You light yourself and become a fire
You give out warmth but you turn to ash
You work hard although your life will become shorter.

Maybe you are just a small fire
But you try your best till the end
Darkness has gone 'cause you are here.

Every 'tear' you make is love
It reminds us the time is gone forever
The rest of our life should never waste time.

You always work in different places
But you only have one purpose
It's to help people, it's to light.

Because of you, we can work at night
Because of you, we know we should not waste time
Because of you, we know we should help people with our power.

The fire of you lights our heart
You are leading us in your spirit
Candle, candle, we thank you
And we love you.

Tim Zeng (14)
The Oratory School, Reading

The Sea

The glittering sea
So precious and free
The rolling waves
Are the ocean's slave

The waves do reach
The wet and sandy beach
Where seals and eels
Wait to catch their meals.

Ben Henderson (14)
The Oratory School, Reading

World War II

The war is long-winded, bullets flying everywhere
Screams and shouts fill the air
I fight for pride and peace, not love and hate.

As the night falls, we know light will be back
Twelve hours to be exact
If I shoot, will that make me a man? Nah!
That's a dare
War is not a game of luck, but one of tactics.

As we move in closer and closer
We hear the sound of drunks and a German song
I fight for pride and peace, not love and hate.

We pause, ready to pounce
But oh no, not for long
War is not a game of luck, but one of tactics.

Bang! Bang! As quick as a flash we clear them out
We feel ashamed and do the sign of the Cross
I fight for pride and peace, not love and hate
War is not a game of luck, but one of tactics.

Will Brazil (13)
The Oratory School, Reading

The Girl Of This Poem

The girl of this poem
Is funny as can be
As kind as candy
Smaller than a palm tree.

She likes to make you laugh
As fun as a playful kitten
She likes to sing in the bath
And washes herself with a mitten.

She loves to cook and eat her food
But keeping her eye on fat
To keep her figure nice and trim
She feeds it to the cat.

She goes on holiday every year
To get her white body brown
It's no good staying in cloudy Britain
Because you never get a tan in the town.

Genevieve Dashwood-Simpson (13)
Tower House School, Paignton

Bombs And Terror

The darkness flies over the light,
Bringing German invaders at night.
From peace to horror, the sky turns grey,
Sirens go off, warning people away.
Blackouts drawn, no chink of light,
Bombs hit houses, people take flight.
So many are dying, the rich and the poor,
Who will end this infernal war?
As daylight comes we see the devastation,
All this to stop the German invasion.

Rachael Craig (12)
Tower House School, Paignton

Growing Up

T ime to go to beddy-byes
E ver so excited
R eady, as always
I know that she is coming
A nd so I close my eyes
N ow I can feel my pillow rising gently
N ever gets old
E very time she has to go -

L ots of beautiful sounds I hear
O h well, another one will soon fall out
U ntil next time, goodbye my precious little fairy
I can't wait to see you again
S oon another is hidden under my pillow
E verything is still in the same place when I wake up

H ow come it is still there and no surprise?
A nybody know where she is?
M aybe she was busy
M aybe she forgot
E ven though she didn't come, I still have money in my bank
T ime to go to work now
T o earn the money I never got that night!

Terianne Louise Hammett (12)
Tower House School, Paignton

Black

A dark gloom that breaks the happiness,
The emptiness of the misty, quiet sky.
A painful time of sorrow and woe.
Bats screeching in the windswept trees,
A depressing moment in the graveyard of death.

Samantha Rainbird (13)
Tower House School, Paignton

Acrostic Poem

H annah
A
N aughty child
N ever wanting to grow up
A ble to tear pages of imaginative text
H urting whenever told off

K eeping childish dreams
A t
T imes that are
E ver so sad

B elieving Santa will come
L eaving empty glasses
A nd sooty footprints
N ever did I think that
C hildren's parents can be so cruel letting us
H ope
A nd now
R egret, but still strong determination
D addy isn't Santa, is he?

Hannah Kate Blanchard (12)
Tower House School, Paignton

Gerrard

G errard the great
E lectrifying pace
R oar! The ball flies wildly past the keeper
R ampaging all over the opposition
A lways scoring terrific goals
R ealising he *has* to win
D eep inside him he cries when he loses.

James Wan (13)
Tower House School, Paignton

Diamante Poem

Fun,
Happy, occupied,
Cheerful, amused, joyful,
Entertaining, jolly, offhand, uninterested,
Fatigued, dim, annoyed,
Depressed, dull,
Bored.

Rob Vaughan (13)
Tower House School, Paignton

First Love - Cinquain

Hot flush
Heart beats faster
Butterflies in stomach
He leans forward, his lips touch mine
First kiss.

Katherine Drew (15)
Tower House School, Paignton

My Wedding - Cinquain

Ding-dong
Confetti falls
I walk down the long aisle
We exchange our gold wedding rings
'I do.'

Harlie Steward (12)
Tower House School, Paignton

Our History Teacher, Mr Doolally

Our history teacher is quite near death
He doesn't even notice when I talk to my mate, Beth
He is aged around ninety-three
And he can't tell the difference between a lamp post and a tree
You might have thought he would have retired and flown free

like a dove

But he has always told us teaching history is his love
Now I have been told the old man is dead
He died so quietly snuggled up in bed
Now we have to have a brand new teacher
Probably someone who is such a preacher
Trying to get information in our head
But we will obviously forget it when we go to bed
I think I will really miss Mr Doolally
The man who lived deep down in a valley
He really did love Devon
But now I know he is way up in Heaven.

Leanne Endacott (12)
Tower House School, Paignton

Hey There, My Baby Boy

Hey there, my baby boy
You fill my life with pride and joy
For you I'd run a whole mile
Just to see your lovely smile
I thank you for the things you've done
You make my life so much fun
Your light is shining like a dove
Because you're filled with so much love
I just want to let you know
I don't want to let you go
This poem is a piece of art
To let you know you'll always be in my heart.

Hannah Griffiths (12)
Tower House School, Paignton

McDonald's

If you eat McDonald's every day
You know there's gonna be a price to pay
Those McFlurrys may taste lush
But actually they're a load of mush.

If you eat McDonald's every day
Your weight won't go, it'll just stay
Burgers, chips and a large Coke too
It will really make you need the loo.

If you eat McDonald's every day
Think to yourself and I will say
If you keep eating you'll be obese
And soon you'll need an extra large fleece.

If you eat McDonald's every day
You'll get fat by the end of May
If you keep on stuffing stuff in your cheeks
You'll start hanging round with a load of freaks.

I can see what lies ahead
And it ain't pretty, cos you will be dead!

Meghan Callaghan (12)
Tower House School, Paignton

Black

The evil, lonely thinker,
Planning his destruction,
The terror, the fright, the pain,
All in one brain,
Never spoken to anyone,
Never had a friend,
Alone in the cold, icy mist,
Vicious eyes, vicious face,
Ruthlessly cold as the ice in his heart,
Skin as pale as paper,
Human blood resting on the mouth.

Charlie Tripp (12)
Tower House School, Paignton

The Writer Of This Poem

(Based on 'The Writer Of This Poem' by Roger McGough)

The writer of this poem
Isn't as strong as an ox
She's not a model
With long, luscious locks.

She doesn't have the best fashion sense
Crazy colours are cool
She loves 'The Simpsons'
And she enjoys school.

She isn't the most popular
Who really is?
She has no one to hold
No one to kiss.

But she belongs to a group of friends
Who stick by her side
Love her for who she is
High and low tide.

Poppy Guest (15)
Tower House School, Paignton

The Beautiful Rose

The blood-red rose,
Strikes a pose,
Its beauty beyond compare,
Its perfume lingers in the evening air!

If I'm happy or if I'm sad,
One glance at a rose and I feel so glad,
For a rose is quite divine and rare,
They are mostly for true lovers to share,
Enchanting is the single rose!

Eliza Dendle (11)
Tower House School, Paignton

Creating A Poem

In a room full of silence
And an empty space
Room for an idea
Full of rhythm and pace

A door in the corner
Slowly creaks as it moves
And in comes a horse
With bright yellow hooves

As my hand starts to jot
Down the horse on my sheet
In strides a monkey
With bright yellow feet

And with my pen
The monkey I draw
When in explodes a camel,
A pigeon and a boar

A whole menagerie
Of imaginary beasts
A party among animals
And the poem is complete.

Oliver Pfaff (15)
Tower House School, Paignton

Red - Haiku

Like dark, fresh red blood,
Gushing from a open wound,
Trickling down my leg.

Shannon Philpott (12)
Tower House School, Paignton

Perfection

Goddamn spots
Pop up here and there!
Greasy skin, greasy hair,
Legs like tree trunks, I can't wear a . . .
Skirt!
Wouldn't be seen
Dead in shorts!
How 'bout a dress?
No, what a mess!
I'm
Nothing
Compared to some girls,
Who know they have it sorted,
Not one flaw in sight,
Nothing wrong or distorted!
How lucky some girls are
Always to look like a star,
Never a hair out of place!
Perfect personality,
Perfect face!

Freya Selley (15)
Tower House School, Paignton

Wind

It moans like a ghost in an open space,
It howls through the doors in great haste,
It blows with great power over the trees,
Scattering twigs, branches and leaves,
It whistles through my window as I cower in bed,
I lift my duvet and bury my head.

Philippa Bowerman (13)
Tower House School, Paignton

Keep On Running

I don't know if you tap your feet,
I almost always do!
For if you don't and won't keep up,
Then death will capture you!

For when you go to sleep at night,
Don't you ever stop,
Just keep on running all the time,
Don't let your tempo drop!

If you wake up in the morn,
A gash across your chest,
You had a stop, you let it lie,
Grim Reaper did the rest . . .

Joshua Callaghan (14)
Tower House School, Paignton

Struggle

I struggled with poetry at the start
It just didn't seem to fit my part
My brain went dead when the word 'poetry' was said
And I thought an E would settle for me.

But through perseverance
And effort
I finally broke the mould
I got the gist
With the help of Miss
So now an A
Is on its way!

Katy Cooper (15)
Tower House School, Paignton

Young Writers Information

We hope you have enjoyed reading this book - and that you will continue to enjoy it in the coming years.

If you like reading and writing poetry drop us a line, or give us a call, and we'll send you a free information pack.

Alternatively if you would like to order further copies of this book or any of our other titles, then please give us a call or log onto our website at www.youngwriters.co.uk

Young Writers Information
Remus House
Coltsfoot Drive
Peterborough
PE2 9JX

(01733) 890066